**#1 INTERNATIONAL BEST SELLER**

# *e*volvepreneur
## *After Hours*
### Show VOL.1

Includes Podcast Guest Directory

# EvolvePreneur® (After Hours) Show Volume 1
### #1 International Best Seller
### By

**John North** opens the book with his deep understanding of the entrepreneurial landscape, providing a narrative that connects the diverse wisdom of the authors.

**Mechelle McDonald** shares her journey in "Podcasting The Future," where she discusses her role as a communicator, entrepreneur, and growth coach, emphasizing the power of impactful conversations.

**Richard Wray** in "Don't Mention The Matrix - How A.I. is Democratising Paranoia and Opportunity," offers a unique perspective on Artificial Intelligence, sharing his journey from a small mining town to collaborations with tech giants.

**Christine Campbell Rapin**, in "Get More Podcast Guest Invitations with These 5 Strategies," provides strategic insights into business growth, drawing from her vast experience in marketing, sales, and operations.

**David Kitchen (Coach Kitch)** shares his expertise in sport psychology and leadership in "Laying Bricks: Building a Business Foundation," focusing on developing leaders and cultivating a success-oriented mindset.

**Manny Skevofilax** in "Profitable Growth Is Achievable," provides essential financial strategies, highlighting the importance of sustainable and profitable growth in business.

**Tamara Pflug** offers practical advice in "Self-Coach for Business Growth," focusing on self-coaching techniques for personal and professional development.

**Tony Pisanelli** explores personal branding and career development in "Career By Design." His insights offer valuable strategies for those looking to craft a successful career path.

**#1 INTERNATIONAL BEST SELLER**

# evolvepreneur
## After Hours Show VOL.1

Includes Podcast Guest Directory

https://evolvepreneur.app/s/afterhours

MECHELLE MCDONALD   JOHN NORTH
CHRISTINE CAMPBELL RAPIN   RICHARD WRAY
MANNY SKEVOFILAX   DAVID KITCHEN
TONY PISANELLI   TAMARA PFLUG

© **Copyright 2024**
By JOHN NORTH and Mechelle McDonald, Richard Wray, Christine Campbell, Rapin, David Kitchen (Coach Kitch), Tony Pisanelli, Tamara Pflug, Manny Skevofilax

Edited by James North
All rights reserved.
Evolvepreneur® is a registered trademark of Evolvepreneur Pty Ltd.

Book Layout ©2023
www.EvolveGlobalPublishing.com

No part of this book may be reproduced or transmitted in any form or by any means, electronic or mechanical, including photocopying, recording or by any information storage and retrieval system, without written permission from the authors, except for the inclusion of brief quotations in a review.

**Limit of Liability Disclaimer:** The information contained in this book is for information purposes only, and may not apply to your situation. The author, publisher, distributor, and provider provide no warranty about the content or accuracy of the content enclosed. The information provided is subjective. Keep this in mind when reviewing this guide. Neither the Publisher nor the Author shall be liable for any loss of profit or any other commercial damages resulting from the use of this guide. All links are for information purposes only and are not warranted for content, accuracy, or any other implied or explicit purpose.

**Earnings Disclaimer:** All income examples in this book are examples. They are not intended to represent or guarantee that everyone will achieve the same results. You understand that each individual's success will be determined by his or her desire, dedication, background, effort, and motivation to work. There is no guarantee you will duplicate any of the results stated here. You recognize any business endeavours have inherent risk or loss of capital.

**Evolvepreneur® (After Hours) Show Volume 1**
1st Edition. 2023 - v5
Font: Georgia
Page size: 6" x 9"

ASIN: B0CQL1KSYV (Amazon Kindle)
ISBN: 978-0-6486232-5-0 (Amazon Print)
ISBN: 978-0-6486232-9-8 (Amazon Hardcover)
ISBN: 978-0-6486232-6-7 (Ingram Spark) PAPERBACK
ISBN: 978-0-6486232-7-4 (Ingram Spark) HARDCOVER
ISBN: 978-0-6486232-4-3 (Smashwords)

CONTACT THE AUTHOR:
Business Name: EVOLVEPRENEUR® PTY LTD
Author Website: www.johnnorth.com.au
Main Website: www.podcastsecrets.biz
All In One Platform: www.evolvepreneur.app
LinkedIn: https://au.linkedin.com/in/johnnorth1085
Twitter: @johnnorth7 and @evolvepreneur

Contact:
Email: info@evolvepreneur.app
Phone: 1300 889 383

**TRADEMARKS**

All product names, logos, and brands are the property of their respective owners. All company, product, and service names used in this book are for identification purposes only. Using these names, logos, and brands does not imply endorsement. All other trademarks cited herein are the property of their respective owners.

# TABLE OF CONTENTS

Launch Your Podcast Show in Minutes! .................................................... 1

Foreword .................................................................................................... 3

About The Authors .................................................................................... 5

Chapter 1 - Podcasting The Future by John North ................................... 7

Chapter 2 - Elevate Your Podcast Experience with these
6 Tips to Becoming An Engaging Podcast Host
by Mechelle McDonald ........................................................ 19

Chapter 3 - Don't Mention The Matrix - How A.I. is
Democratising Paranoia and Opportunity
by Richard Wray ................................................................... 27

Chapter 4 - Get More Podcast Guest Invitations with
These 5 Strategies by Christine Campbell Rapin ................ 41

Chapter 5 - Laying Bricks: Building a Business
Foundation by David Kitchen .............................................. 51

Chapter 6 - Profitable Growth Is Achievable by Manny Skevofilax ........ 65

Chapter 7 - Self-Coach for Business Growth by Tamara Pflug ............... 77

Chapter 8 - Career By Design by Tony Pisanelli ..................................... 91

Podcast Guest Directory ......................................................................... 103
    Growth ................................................................................................ 105
    Leadership .......................................................................................... 121
    Marketing ........................................................................................... 125
    Mindset ............................................................................................... 135
    Strategy .............................................................................................. 139
    Success ............................................................................................... 143

# LAUNCH YOUR PODCAST SHOW IN MINUTES!

Powerful Yet Simple "All in One" Podcast Solution Launch Your Podcast Show in Minutes!

Create or transfer your own podcast to your Evolvepreneur platform and handle every aspect of it in one place. No messy hosting issues or complex setup.

**BUILD YOUR SHOW PAGE IN 2 MINUTES**   **EASILY MANAGE AND PROMOTE YOUR GUESTS**   **GROW SUBSCRIBERS WITH AUTO OFFERS AND ALERTS**

### Why Should You Use PodcastSecrets.biz?

Designed to not only help you create and set up an awesome podcast, but we also help you focus on how to grow your audience and revenues at the same time

### Subscribers Signup and Episode Alerts

Ability to have email subscribers and alert them automatically when a new episode comes out. Almost no-one does this and if they do they never give you the email addresses.

### Take Advantage of Our Done With You Service

We handle the entire process from start to finish and ensure you launch a successful Podcast.

### Setup & Design

The setup phase where we will design your show page and artwork and create your show pages. As well we will help design your subscriber and guest process.

### Awesome Podcast Show Page

Your show page is a central page to send all your traffic and keep your listeners informed and up-to-date. Our easy Podcast Settings page lets you customise your show page and set your show up for distribution.

### Automated Guest Handling Process

We make it easy for you to manage guests for your show. We even have a system for them to apply to be on your show and then work through a process before the interview and record all in one place!

### Strategic Advice

Using our specialised knowledge we can help create a targeted and well designed concept.

### Go Live (Launch and Grow)

We show you how to create episodes and manage the day to day operations for your show.

Learn More at www.podcastsecrets.biz

EvolvePreneur® After Hours Show Vol. 1

Listen here: www.evolvepreneursecrets.show

# FOREWORD
## by John North

Hello and welcome to "Evolvepreneur Secrets," a collection of insights and wisdom from some of the most innovative and inspiring entrepreneurs around the globe.

I'm John North, and it's my privilege to introduce you to a few of our remarkable authors, each bringing their unique perspectives and expertise to this compilation.

First, we have Mechelle McDonald, a multifaceted communicator from The Bahamas. Mechelle is an entrepreneur, growth coach, and skilled speaker and writer. Her work, including hosting the culturally rich show "Vibration" and the Evolvepreneur (After Hours) Show podcast, showcases her passion for empowering others through impactful conversations. Mechelle's commitment extends to community outreach, and she is the proud owner of AmberL, an artisan skincare company in The Bahamas.

Next, meet Richard Wray, an entrepreneur who's making strides in the field of Artificial Intelligence. Hailing from a small mining town in Northern England, Richard's journey to working with major companies like Microsoft and the BBC is nothing short of inspiring. He hosts "The Evolvepreneur A.I. Advantage" podcast, where he engages in insightful discussions about democratizing opportunities and demystifying A.I.. Richard's approach to technology is infused with a social conscience, making his insights invaluable.

Then, there's Christine Campbell Rapin, the CEO of CLEAR Acceleration Inc. With over 25 years of experience in marketing, sales, and operations, Christine has worked with over 400 businesses worldwide, generating combined revenues exceeding one billion dollars. She's a sought-after mentor, guiding business owners to create profitable and impactful ventures. Christine's approach to business growth is strategic, emphasizing efficiency and effectiveness.

Finally, I'd like to introduce David Kitchen, also known as Coach Kitch. As the Founder and President of Edge Leadership Academy, he brings a wealth of experience from his time as a Division 1 Coach and his expertise in sports psychology. His work in building leaders, culture, and mindset in both sports and business is exemplary. Coach Kitch is an award-winning speaker, consultant, and coach trusted by CEOs and high performers across various fields.

Each author in this book brings a wealth of knowledge and experience, offering valuable insights into the world of entrepreneurship. I am excited for you to dive into their stories and learn from their journeys. Enjoy "Evolvepreneur Secrets"!

In addition to the insightful chapters from our featured authors, I'm thrilled to share another special component of this book – our comprehensive podcast guest directory. This directory is a testament to the diverse and rich conversations that have taken place on the Evolvepreneur Podcast Show.

Our podcast has been a vibrant platform for over 300 guests, each bringing unique experiences, knowledge, and insights. This directory is a valuable resource, connecting you with a wide range of thought leaders, innovators, and entrepreneurs who have graced our show. From industry experts to groundbreaking start-up founders, the directory encompasses a spectrum of voices that have contributed to the dynamic discussions on our podcast.

Each guest has shared their journey, challenges, and triumphs, offering practical advice and inspiring stories. The directory lists these incredible individuals and provides a gateway to explore their work further. Whether you're looking for inspiration, guidance, or a fresh perspective, this directory is a treasure trove of entrepreneurial wisdom.

As you delve into the chapters of "Evolvepreneur Secrets," I encourage you also to explore the podcast guest directory. It's an opportunity to extend your learning and connect with a community of like-minded individuals passionate about making a difference in the world of entrepreneurship.

Enjoy the journey through the pages of this book and the many voices that have contributed to the Evolvepreneur community!

# ABOUT THE AUTHORS

### John North

John, the curator of "Evolvepreneur (After Hours) Show - Volume 1," is renowned in the entrepreneurial community. His expertise spans a wide range of business domains, and he is known for his ability to weave diverse entrepreneurial narratives into a cohesive and compelling anthology.

### Mechelle McDonald

Mechelle is a multifaceted entrepreneur, growth coach, and communicator from The Bahamas. Her expertise lies in empowering others through engaging conversations and community outreach. As a host of the show "Vibration" and the Evolvepreneur (After Hours) Show podcast, Mechelle has significantly impacted the entrepreneurial community.

### Richard Wray

Richard's journey from a small mining town in Northern England to becoming a key player in the field of Artificial Intelligence is nothing short of inspiring. His work with major companies like Microsoft and the BBC showcases his ability to bridge the gap between complex technology and practical business applications.

### Christine Campbell Rapin

With over 25 years of experience in marketing, sales, and operations, Christine is a force to be reckoned with in the business world. As the CEO of CLEAR Acceleration Inc., she has worked with over 400 businesses globally, contributing to revenues exceeding one billion dollars.

### David Kitchen (Coach Kitch)

David, known as Coach Kitch, brings a wealth of experience from his time as a Division 1 Coach and his expertise in sports psychology. As the Founder and President of Edge Leadership Academy, he has made significant contributions to the fields of leadership and mindset development.

### Manny Skevofilax

Manny is a financial strategist who brings a wealth of knowledge and expertise to the table, particularly in the realm of achieving sustainable and profitable business growth.

### Tamara Pflug

Tamara is an expert in personal development and entrepreneurial success. Her focus on self-coaching techniques provides a unique perspective in the entrepreneurial world. Tamara's approach is centered on empowering individuals to harness their inner strengths and capabilities.

### Tony Pisanelli

Tony is a seasoned expert in career development and personal branding. His insights and strategies are grounded in extensive experience, helping individuals shape their professional journeys and build successful careers.

Listen here: www.evolvepreneursecrets.show

Chapter 1

# PODCASTING THE FUTURE

**John North**

## About John North

John North is a distinguished figure in the entrepreneurial world, renowned for his extensive and multifaceted career. He is a nine-time #1 International Best Selling Author, celebrated for his works that span various domains, including book publishing, business strategy, internet marketing, and even a book about squash. His reputation as a versatile and experienced entrepreneur is built on a solid foundation in accounting, banking, business management, finance, personal development, IT, software, and strategic marketing.

As the CEO of Evolve Systems Group, John has established himself as a serial entrepreneur, spearheading numerous innovative products and services designed to empower business owners and entrepreneurs. His ventures primarily focus on book publishing and software systems, reflecting his dedication to making a tangible difference in the entrepreneurial community. Some of his notable ventures include Evolve Global Publishing, Evolvepreneur.app, Evolve Your Business, and Evolve Mobile.

John is deeply passionate about helping business owners enhance their marketing intelligence and strategies. He is known for constantly pushing the boundaries of what's possible in today's fast-paced business world and is acclaimed among his peers for his inventive and highly creative problem-solving approach. Through Evolve Global Publishing, John has created a premium service that enables him to assist thousands of entrepreneurs. He emphasizes the importance of implementation and accountability in achieving success. He has developed methodologies that allow entrepreneurs to create and publish their books in as little as 90 days without writing a single word.

His latest venture, Evolvepreneur.app, is an all-in-one platform that empowers entrepreneurs to take control of their future and reduce their reliance on social media for managing their business online. This platform reflects John's commitment to providing comprehensive solutions that cater to the evolving needs of modern entrepreneurs.

John's achievements and contributions to the entrepreneurial world testify to his expertise, innovation, and commitment to fostering growth and success in the entrepreneurial community.

## The Genesis of a Vision

My journey into the world of podcasting was not a sudden leap but a thoughtful transition fueled by a burning desire to create a platform that would resonate with entrepreneurs globally. This venture was inspired by the insights I gained from writing "Podcasting Secrets for Entrepreneurs," a #1 International Best Selling book that introduced me to the world of podcasting and helped shape my vision.

In the early stages, I spent countless hours conceptualizing the purpose of the Evolvepreneur (After Hours) Show. I envisioned a podcast that would go beyond mere business discussions, aiming to delve into entrepreneurs' stories, challenges, and triumphs. It was about creating a space that fostered learning, inspiration, and connection.

I finally came up with this as a statement of who the show was for:

*"As a time-poor, typically underfunded online entrepreneur who receives so much conflicting advice about the best ways to grow your business, how can you compete with the big end of town without any of the resources they have at their disposal?"*

The process involved some planning and strategizing. I reflected on the questions posed in the book:

What unique angle could my podcast offer?

How could it add value to the entrepreneurial community?

What were the stories and insights that needed to be shared?

The answers to these questions formed the foundation of the podcast, guiding its direction and purpose.

Drawing from the book's emphasis on having a clear mission, I crafted a mission statement for the podcast.

This mission statement was more than a few words; it was a guiding principle for every decision, every episode, and every interview. It encapsulated the essence of what I wanted to achieve: to empower, educate, and connect entrepreneurs from all walks of life.

*"Are you a startup entrepreneur or looking to pivot and re-invent your business and struggling with the complexity?*

*The question in my mind is...*

*How do you create or re-launch a highly profitable and successful 6 to 7 figure business?*

*With so much conflicting advice about the best ways to start and grow your business how do you get it right, the first time!"*

## Building the Foundation

The initial phase also involved understanding the podcasting landscape. I immersed myself in learning about different podcast formats, audience engagement strategies, and content themes. This was a period of intense research and learning, where "Podcasting Secrets for Entrepreneurs" served as a critical resource.

I explored various podcasting platforms, delved into the technicalities of podcast production, and studied successful podcasts to understand what made them resonate with their audiences. This comprehensive approach ensured that when I finally launched the Evolvepreneur (After Hours) Show, it was not just another podcast but a well-thought-out platform poised to make a meaningful impact.

The journey of launching the podcast was filled with excitement, challenges, and learning. But armed with a clear vision and guided by the invaluable insights from "Podcasting Secrets for Entrepreneurs," I was ready to embark on this exciting adventure, setting out to create a podcast that would inspire entrepreneurs.

## Crafting a Unique Podcast Identity

### Developing a Distinctive Voice

As the author of "Podcasting Secrets for Entrepreneurs," I understood the critical importance of a podcast's unique identity. The Evolvepreneur (After Hours) Show needed more than just a collection of interviews and discussions; it needed a distinctive voice to make it instantly recognizable to its listeners.

This process involved deep introspection and creative thinking. What did I want the Evolvepreneur brand to represent?

How could the podcast's identity reflect the values and aspirations of the entrepreneurial community it aimed to serve? I sought to create an identity that was memorable and resonated with the core audience of the podcast.

## Visual and Audio Branding

A significant part of creating this identity was visual and audio branding. The logo, color scheme, and overall design aesthetic were carefully chosen to represent the podcast's branding. These elements were not just decorative; they were visual cues that communicated the essence of the Evolvepreneur (After Hours) Show to its audience.

## Consistency Across Episodes

Consistency was key. Each episode, regardless of the topic or guest, needed to align with the overall identity of the podcast. This tone, style, and content consistency helped build a brand that listeners could trust and relate to. As I emphasized in "Podcasting Secrets for Entrepreneurs," consistency in podcasting is not just about regular episode releases; it's also about maintaining a consistent quality and style that becomes your trademark. This was something we spent some time training our hosts to pay attention to when interviewing guests.

## A Unique Blend of Content

The content of the Evolvepreneur (After Hours) Show was designed to reflect its unique identity. We didn't just focus on success stories; we also delved into entrepreneurs' challenges, failures, and real-life experiences. This approach set our podcast apart, making it a source of genuine insight and inspiration for our listeners.

## Diverse Perspectives and Topics

To ensure diversity and richness in our content, I invited guests from various sectors within the entrepreneurial world. This diversity brought different perspectives and experiences to the show, making each episode a unique learning opportunity. We discussed the latest trends in entrepreneurship, shared success stories, and, importantly, talked about failures and the lessons learned from them.

## Creating Engaging and Actionable Content

Each episode was crafted to be engaging and actionable. I wanted listeners to come away with not just insights but also practical tips and strategies they could apply in their own entrepreneurial journeys. This focus on actionable content sets the Evolvepreneur (After Hours) Show apart, making it a valuable resource for our audience.

## Continuous Learning and Adaptation

In line with the teachings of "Podcasting Secrets for Entrepreneurs," I continuously sought feedback from our guests to adapt and evolve our content. This feedback loop was instrumental in keeping our content relevant and engaging. It also helped build a stronger connection with our audience.

Developing content that resonated with our audience was a dynamic and ongoing process. It required understanding the audience, strategic planning, and a commitment to delivering valuable and engaging content. These principles, which I detailed in "Podcasting Secrets for Entrepreneurs," were the cornerstone of our content development strategy and played a significant role in the success of the Evolvepreneur (After Hours) Show.

## Fostering Meaningful Connections with Guests

### The Art of Selecting and Engaging Guests

One of the most vital aspects of the Evolvepreneur (After Hours) Show has been our guests. In "Podcasting Secrets for Entrepreneurs," I discuss the importance of choosing guests who bring value to the podcast and resonate with the audience. Using the Evolvepreneur.app platform, I implemented a systematic approach to identify and engage with potential guests who could offer unique insights and experiences to our listeners.

### Building a Diverse Guest Roster

Diversity in our guest roster was crucial. I aimed to showcase various voices from different backgrounds, industries, and stages of their entrepreneurial journey. This diversity enriched our content, giving listeners a broad spectrum of perspectives and insights. Each guest brought unique stories, challenges, and lessons, making every episode a new and enriching experience.

### Preparation and Research

Preparation and research were key components in making the most of each guest's appearance. Before each interview, I invested time in understanding the guest's background, achievements, and areas of expertise. This preparation allowed for deeper and more meaningful conversations, as highlighted in my

Listen here: www.evolvepreneursecrets.show

book. It also showed respect for our guests' time and contributions, fostering appreciation and mutual respect.

We build an entire "Host Hub" as part of our platform's podcast module to make this a seamless and easy process for our hosts.

## Creating a Comfortable and Open Environment

Creating a comfortable and open environment for our guests was paramount. The Evolvepreneur.app platform facilitated this by streamlining the communication process, making it easy for guests to understand the show's format and what was expected of them. As much of the process as possible happened inside this one platform, making the experience convenient for guests. This clarity and ease of interaction set the stage for open, honest, and engaging conversations.

Guests had their own "Guest Hub" which was designed to give them a central place to track their episode from start to finish as well as provide access to promotional links and resources.

## Leveraging Guest Networks

In addition to the value each guest brought to the podcast regarding content, their networks also significantly expanded our reach. Guests often shared their episodes within their networks, introducing new audiences to the Evolvepreneur (After Hours) Show. This cross-promotion benefited both the podcast and the guests, creating a symbiotic relationship.

We developed an automated email system to let the guest know when their episode was scheduled and when it was released.

These efforts, guided by the principles in "Podcasting Secrets for Entrepreneurs," enhanced the quality of our episodes and played a significant role in the growth and popularity of the Evolvepreneur (After Hours) Show.

## Technical Mastery for Quality Production

## Prioritizing Sound Quality and Production

As I emphasized in "Podcasting Secrets for Entrepreneurs," the technical quality of a podcast can significantly influence its success. For the Evolvepreneur (After Hours) Show, the top priority was prioritizing sound quality and overall production value. Investing in high-quality recording equipment, microphones, and editing software was the first step in this process.

### Setting Up a Professional Recording Environment

Creating a professional recording environment was crucial. I focused on setting up an acoustically sound space that was free from distractions. This environment improved the sound quality and provided a comfortable setting for both myself and the guests, conducive to natural and relaxed conversations.

### Mastering Audio Editing

Audio editing was another critical aspect. Learning and mastering audio editing techniques allowed me to enhance the clarity and quality of each episode. This process involved removing background noises, balancing sound levels, and ensuring a consistent audio experience throughout the podcast. As outlined in my book, attention to these details played a significant role in delivering a professional and enjoyable listening experience.

### Continuous Improvement and Adaptation

Embracing continuous improvement and staying updated with the latest technological advancements was key. I regularly explored new software and equipment that could further enhance the podcast's quality. Adapting to new technologies kept the podcast technically sound and demonstrated a commitment to providing the best possible experience to our audience.

Technical mastery in podcast production was an ongoing learning, adaptation, and investment journey. The focus on high-quality production, as guided by the principles in "Podcasting Secrets for Entrepreneurs," was instrumental in establishing the Evolveprencur (After Hours) Show as a professional and reputable podcast in the entrepreneurial space.

## Monetizing the Podcast Effectively

### Exploring Diverse Revenue Streams

In "Podcasting Secrets for Entrepreneurs," I stress the importance of monetizing a podcast effectively to ensure its sustainability and growth. Exploring diverse revenue streams for the Evolvepreneur (After Hours) Show was a strategic decision. This included sponsorships, affiliate marketing, and leveraging the podcast's content for other products, such as books or online courses.

## Content Repurposing

Repurposing content from the podcast was another effective monetization strategy. This involved turning insightful episodes or series into ebooks, online courses, or exclusive content for premium subscribers. Such initiatives allowed us to reach a broader audience and added value to our listeners.

We have also added shorts of each episode in our Youtube Channel to promote the guests.

## Affiliate Marketing

Affiliate marketing was also integrated into our strategy. By recommending products or services that were relevant and beneficial to our audience, we were able to generate revenue through affiliate commissions. This approach required careful selection to ensure the products and services promoted aligned with our audience's interests and needs.

Building and Nurturing a Loyal Community

## Introducing the VIP Boost Offer

In the journey of podcasting, as I've detailed in "Podcasting Secrets for Entrepreneurs," building and nurturing a community is as crucial as producing content. The Evolvepreneur (After Hours) Show aimed to attract listeners and create an engaged community around it.

To enhance this community-building effort and cover operational costs, we introduced an innovative offering: the VIP Boost Package.

## The VIP Boost Concept

The VIP Boost Package was designed to give our guests an extraordinary experience and additional exposure. Recognizing that every interview is unique, we wanted to offer something extra to make each episode stand out. The package included a series of exclusive benefits:

Facebook Ads Push: We allocated a budget of $100 for Facebook Ads for each VIP episode, ensuring that these episodes received heightened exposure and reached a broader audience. This not only benefited the guests but also brought more listeners to our show.

Original Content Files: VIP guests received the original video and audio interview files. This allowed them to share and repurpose their content, extending the life and reach of their episode.

Custom Promo Video and Images: We provided professionally edited promo videos and images with the guest's headshot. These were tailored to promote the show and the guest, enhancing their personal brand.

Bite-sized Social Media Content: Understanding the power of social media, we created up to three 'reels' from each VIP episode. These short, engaging clips captured attention and drew new listeners to the full episode.

### Why VIP Boost?

The VIP Boost was more than just a monetization strategy; it was a way to add value and elevate the experience for our guests. It distinguished our podcast in a market saturated with content, offering our guests a platform not just to share their story but to truly shine. This approach was aligned with the principles in "Podcasting Secrets for Entrepreneurs," where I emphasize the importance of creating unique value propositions in your podcasting venture.

### Limited and Exclusive Offering

The VIP Boost was a limited offer exclusive to those who were eager to amplify their impact and stand out in the crowd. It was a testament to our commitment to producing quality content and supporting our guests in maximizing their reach and influence.

The VIP Boost Package was a strategic initiative that helped build and nurture our podcast community. It provided additional value to our guests, covered operational costs, and enhanced the overall quality and reach of the Evolvepreneur (After Hours) Show. This innovative approach, inspired by the strategies in "Podcasting Secrets for Entrepreneurs," played a significant role in the growth and success of our podcast.

### Building a Sustainable Revenue Model

The key to successful monetization was building a sustainable revenue model that did not compromise the integrity of the podcast. Each monetization avenue was carefully considered to ensure it aligned with the podcast's mission and provided genuine value to our listeners. This approach, as outlined in "Podcasting Secrets for Entrepreneurs," ensured that our monetization efforts contributed to the overall quality and longevity of the Evolvepreneur (After Hours) Show.

Effectively monetizing the podcast required a multifaceted approach, focusing on sponsorships, content repurposing, and affiliate marketing. These strategies, guided by the principles in "Podcasting Secrets for Entrepreneurs," helped establish a sustainable revenue model that supported the growth and success of the podcast.

## Staying Agile and Adapting to Trends

### Embracing Industry Changes

In the dynamic world of podcasting, staying agile and adaptable is crucial for sustained success. In "Podcasting Secrets for Entrepreneurs," I emphasize the importance of staying attuned to industry trends and technological advancements. For the Evolvepreneur (After Hours) Show, this meant continuously evolving our approach to content creation, marketing, and audience engagement.

### Innovating with New Formats and Technologies

We constantly explored new formats and technologies to keep our content fresh and engaging. This included experimenting with different episode structures, incorporating new audio-visual elements, and utilizing emerging platforms for broader reach. By staying ahead of the curve, we ensured the podcast remained relevant and appealing to a diverse audience.

### Enhancing Accessibility

Part of adapting to trends involved making our content more accessible and inclusive. We looked into ways to make our episodes more enjoyable for a wider range of listeners, including those with different abilities. This included offering transcripts.

Staying agile and adapting to trends was a key factor in the longevity and success of the Evolvepreneur (After Hours) Show. This approach, guided by the principles in "Podcasting Secrets for Entrepreneurs," allowed us to continuously innovate and evolve, keeping our content fresh, relevant, and engaging.

## Encouraging Further Learning

### Promoting Continued Growth and Exploration

In my journey with the Evolvepreneur (After Hours) Show, I've always believed in the power of continuous learning and growth. As highlighted in "Podcasting Secrets for Entrepreneurs," a #1 International Best Selling book, the podcasting landscape is rich with opportunities for exploration and advancement. I encourage aspiring podcasters and entrepreneurs to delve into this book for a deeper understanding and practical guidance.

## A Comprehensive Guide to Podcasting

"Podcasting Secrets for Entrepreneurs" is a comprehensive guide, offering insights into every aspect of podcasting. From conceptualizing and launching a podcast to growing an audience and monetizing effectively, the book covers a wide range of topics essential for anyone looking to succeed in this space.

## Expanding Knowledge Beyond the Podcast

I advocate for expanding one's knowledge beyond just our podcast episodes. The book provides a wealth of information that complements the learnings from the Evolvepreneur (After Hours) Show. It's a resource that can help podcasters at any stage of their journey, whether they are just starting or looking to take their podcast to the next level.

## A Call to Action for Readers

I invite readers and listeners to embrace the teachings of "Podcasting Secrets for Entrepreneurs." This book is not just a collection of tips and strategies; it's a roadmap for building a successful and impactful podcast. With this resource, I believe every voice can find its audience, and every podcast can achieve its potential.

Connect with me

https://evolvepreneur.app/s/johnnorth

Get a FREE Copy of Podcast Secrets for Entrepreneurs

https://evolvepreneur.app/s/podcastbook

Chapter 2

# ELEVATE YOUR PODCAST EXPERIENCE WITH THESE 6 TIPS TO BECOMING AN ENGAGING PODCAST HOST

**Mechelle McDonald**

## About Mechelle McDonald

Mechelle A. McDonald delivers communication that connects beyond borders. A multifaceted communicator, she is a Bahamian writer, entrepreneur, growth coach and speaker.

Mechelle A. McDonald finds joy in empowering and uplifting others through impactful conversations. Mechelle began her hosting career as a guest host on local shows, before finding her cultural educational show Vibration and joining the Australian-based Evolvepreneur (After Hours) Show podcast, one of the top 5% podcasts worldwide as a top host. With a love for her Bahamian background, Vibration provides a platform for Bahamian and Afro-Caribbean advocates and visionaries to share their unique perspectives on history, culture and identity.

Within her hosting career, she has created captivating conversations with over 170 global speakers, including 6 and 7-figure CEOs, coaches, consultants, advocates and visionaries. As a speaker, her audience has included seniors, teens, adult learners, and business owners throughout the Caribbean. In addition to speaking, Mechelle also served as a panellist and moderator for in-person and virtual seminars, webinars and talking sessions.

She has received recognition for her passion for community outreach, motivating others, and living a purposeful life that creates impact. A part of this is volunteering in a local feeding program and writing a case study that raised awareness of wildlife trafficking, which was also a part of an international course to prevent this heinous act. Known for her involvement in initiatives, Mechelle believes in bridging the gap for those in need and uses her voice to bring power to others.

Her business, AmberL, an artisan skincare company in The Bahamas, provides a safe space for individuals with skin conditions, which includes providing natural solutions and an environment of trust to share their skin stories. She is also the Madecraft author of the highly rated LinkedIn Learning course, Setting a Vision: How to Gain Clarity on Your Goals, which has reached over 3,000 global learners.

**My Seasons:**

https://evolvepreneur.app/podcast/category/season-four-mechelle
https://evolvepreneur.app/podcast/category/season-six-mechelle

Listen here: www.evolvepreneursecrets.show

Mechelle McDonald

Conversations are among the most universal ways to create bonds, share information and leave impressions that last a lifetime. Whether brief or extended, all conversations create a level of impact that is both priceless and serves as a life lesson in some shape or form. Podcasting has revolutionized how we consume audio content and has become the go-to for information dissemination in the digital world. As a podcast host, you have the ability to not only lead the conversations with your guests but also elevate your impact on them and your audience. It's a privilege to have this ability and one that is an asset to your brand and your guests' overall experience.

According to demandsage.com, in 2023, it's noted that podcasting is a $23+ billion-dollar industry, and there are 464.7 million podcast listeners worldwide. With five million podcasts available globally, wouldn't you want to incorporate steps to help your podcast stand out and elevate your podcast experience for guests and listeners alike? In this chapter, I'll share with you the growth that led to podcast hosting and some essential tips that have elevated my podcasting experience as a sought-after host.

Would you believe that I grew up being an introvert? Yes, I was the quiet girl in school. I rarely socialized growing up, and I was not one to freely express my opinion or stand in the spotlight. Becoming a multi-faceted communicator was a role that I evolved into over the years, and each enhanced skill allowed me to connect with my audiences more.

I began my communications journey as a poet. My mother, Norma, a poet, constantly supported the beautiful gift she had passed on to me. She excitedly and wholeheartedly shared my poem "Christmas" with family and friends during the Christmas Holiday. It was such an elaborate event, with the poem beautifully printed on a light paper that rolled up like scrolls. It was one of the greatest pieces ever written to her, and I felt the same because of her love and encouragement. Being a young writer and reader fostered my love for learning new words and their definitions, which stayed with me through high school, where I was a constant spelling bee entry who primarily loved receiving the new word list over actual competing.

My writing evolved from poetry to writing feature articles (based on food and fashion) for local magazines such as Bahamas Tourism Weekly and Exiles Magazine, with the latter highlighting a feature article on the guest designer of Islands of the World Fashion Week guest designer and Project Runway Season 1 champion, Jay McCarroll. Personal blogging and press releases followed with online and print media publications, including The Tribune newspaper and The Bahamas Weekly (.com) and corporate blog posts for US-based clients.

My love of writing and reading created the foundation for building my vocabulary with ease. Is it surprising that I won the Linguist award in my first Toastmasters International club? It was easy to apply these to improve my speaking skills once I overcame the nervousness. Even though my confidence has grown, I'm still aware of how uneasy the stage can feel in the first few seconds.

Speaking allows for voice projection and expressing your concept and idea in a way that's uniquely your own. In public speaking, you control the narrative and can emphasize specific aspects of your message. I enjoy presenting at speaking engagements and am thankful to create an impact on local and international audiences through it.

By embarking on course creation, I've intertwined my speaking, writing, hosting, and reading experience to provide education and insight for global learners of any age. This onsite US-based experience elevated my presentation and on-camera skills. It resulted in a personal growth and self-development course with top e-learning platforms, Cornerstone and LinkedIn Learning.

With a love for my Bahamian culture, I founded and hosted the show Vibration, which provides a platform for Bahamian and Afro-Caribbean advocates, entrepreneurs, doctors and visionaries (70 to date). This online platform allowed guests to speak their distinct truth, passion and personal message to a global audience and create a ripple impact. In addition to my fellow Bahamians, the show has featured guests from Guyana, West Africa, and Trinidad & Tobago.

Joining the Evolvepreneur (After Hours) Show podcast in late 2022, I've captivated audiences with intriguing conversations with over 100 global speakers, including six and seven-figure CEOs, coaches, consultants, authors, and entrepreneurs. Each guest provided unique insights into businesses of any level. Having inspired and been inspired by my guests, I received five-star reviews for creating a space for guests to feel relaxed and open to sharing their stories.

I'm among the top requested hosts, with my first season garnering over 22k views and an average of 450 views per episode (https://evolvepreneur.app/podcast/category/season-four-mechelle). This continues to be one of my most rewarding career experiences.

Listen here: www.evolvepreneursecrets.show

Based on my professional experience, here are six tips to advance your skills as a podcast host and build a reputation for creating a welcoming space for inspiring, insightful and open conversation.

## Be Yourself

If you are naturally curious, funny, talkative or witty, include these personal traits in your podcast host personality. If you like comedy, start with a funny statement. If you are a literature fan, end each episode with a philosophical quote or saying. If you love art, infuse it into your background, the title of your podcast or even an aspect of your attire.

Let the guest and audience know exactly who you are by incorporating it into your hosting. As the podcast host, you are a fundamental aspect of the show's brand, and your audience's (as well as guests') interest will rely on how you present yourself during the show. Align your traits to the podcast's focus; it will become a signature part of the brand and why viewers tune in and subscribe.

## Know Your Guest

This is one of the key aspects of engaging with your guests and your audience. Take the time to research your guest to understand their background, business, motivation and goals. This will include reviewing their personal or professional website, biography, books they've written or co-authored, podcasts or other contributions that display who they are and what they believe. Showing your guest that you took the time to research and understand them shows a sign of respect and appreciation for them and their contributions. It removes the awkwardness of feeling like strangers. It reminds the guests that the focus is on them and that you value them as a guest. This also helps them to feel relaxed and comfortable during the recording. This is an integral part of your episode preparation.

## Develop an Episode Layout

After researching your guests and becoming more familiar with who they are as individuals, you now have the tools to create an outline for your episode. Here, you would include the following:

- ▶ Your podcast's opening (key phrase or statement that connects to the show's purpose and introduces you as the host, show sponsors, topic, etc.). The opening should align with the mission and vision of the show, providing clarity on what to expect per episode and within the season. Ensure that your opening instantly captures the audience's attention and maintains their interest.

- Guest's introduction (a brief introduction of your guest highlighting key points about the guest and their background, preferably pre-approved by them). This can include their business, origin, academic and professional experience, personal quotes or beliefs and current ventures.
- Questions that connect to the show and guests. This is where your research shines! Develop questions, allowing your guests to speak on topics they like and are familiar with. This can range from business to personal topics that provide insight for your audience and add credibility to your show. Share the layout with your guests at least two days in advance so they know what to expect and are not caught off guard with questions that make them uneasy.

## Include Voice Intonation

Have you ever been in a seminar or conference where the presenter uses a steady tone throughout their session?

You (and other audience members) will quickly lose focus and interest in their message, even if it's groundbreaking!

The average attention span of an individual is 8.25 seconds (*https://www.thetreetop.com/statistics/average-human-attention-span*) meaning that it's critical to maintain the guests' and audience's interests within seconds.

Incorporating voice intonation—which is the rise and fall of your voice's tone—is essential to capture interest. This allows you to emphasize keywords, infuse emotions into your words as you speak and communicate empathy by lowering your tone.

This will also allow your questions and the episode to be received more quickly. To practice this, take a six-word sentence, and each time you say the sentence, place emphasis on one word that reflects a sense of emotion and depth in the meaning of the word. This will allow you to understand how the tone used per word can change its definition upon speaking. You can also take ten words neutrally at first, then again with a rise in your voice and then a lowering of your voice (but not with bass).

## Keep it Conversational

Firstly, as a host, it is natural to feel nervous, especially if it is your first time. This nervousness will decrease over time. As nervous as you may be, know that your guests are often also nervous, so let's keep it conversational! To keep the dialogue conversational:

- It's important to start the dialogue with something heartfelt, funny, or easily relatable (a personal experience, funny moment, etc.).
- Talk as though you're speaking with a friend, but keep it professional.
- Ask questions freely (that connect with the guest and topic). You want to keep your guests feeling at ease and knowing they can express themselves freely and without judgment. This helps them to open up and remove any tension.

**Active Listening and Interaction**

Active listening involves truly listening to your guest and their message by:

- Listen to keywords or phrases as feedback and reiterate to show mutual understanding and allow for deeper insight. This creates an open door for the guest to expand on the referenced point with examples of their experiences or words of wisdom to encourage the audience.
- Commenting or asking questions on topics the guest shows more interest or comfort in mentioning before or throughout the episode. As the host, you want to remove the notion of feeling like they're on a stage or to give perfect responses. As the host, you guide the conversation while allowing room for the guests to fully express themselves so that they, too, have a positive experience. I have had guests who expressed joy and a sigh of relief because they thoroughly enjoyed feeling welcomed and listened to. They said it was either their first podcast guest experience or their best experience.
- Supporting and following their journey throughout the conversation through verbal and non-verbal language (nodding, clapping, speaking in agreeance, etc.). This is a crucial step in your guests knowing that you are experiencing and walking through the conversation with them, allowing them not to feel alone. It boosts their confidence and helps to reduce anxiety.
- Responding appropriately by being mindful of when a topic or phrase is mentioned that requires a response that shows compassion, care, understanding and empathy when needed. This shows consideration towards the emotions and experiences of the guest. This connects to the humanistic side of podcasting and removes the focus from merely creating an episode from a business perspective.

Incorporating these six tips will elevate your hosting skills, the dialogue quality of each episode, the interaction with your guests, and your on-camera experience. The more you practice these, the more your podcast episodes will improve.

These tips apply to hosts within the first 1 – 3 years of their podcast or those who are experiencing difficulty connecting with their guests and audience. Being an engaging podcast host will make the experience more rewarding for you, the guest and the audience while also leading to more positive reviews.

You will also grow as a communicator and be able to create more interactive conversations both on and off-camera. You will also find that by being more focused on highlighting, supporting and listening to your guests, you are more likely to receive guest referrals to your show, which can be converted to leads.

As a podcast host, never lose sight of why you started the show, and remember the value of keeping your guests (and audience) at the center by keeping them engaged, motivated, and seen. This vision will allow you to constantly evolve as a host, grow with your brand and provide numerous captivating experiences.

Connect with me

*https://evolvepreneur.app/s/mechelle*

Chapter 3

# DON'T MENTION THE MATRIX - HOW A.I. IS DEMOCRATISING PARANOIA AND OPPORTUNITY

**Richard Wray**

## About Richard Wray

Richard is a host on the Evolvepreneur (After Hours) Show with over 90 episodes and counting, showcasing his deep engagement in the world of entrepreneurship and technology.

Originating from a modest mining town in the North of England, Richard has surpassed expectations, working and living in various countries and contributing to the success of major corporations like Microsoft, the BBC, and BSkyB. Defying early scepticism, he has carved out a remarkable career path. Currently, he's an entrepreneur in the field of Artificial Intelligence, focusing on applying technology with a social conscience.

Richard's passion for AI and entrepreneurship is also evident in his consultant role and the host of his podcast, 'The Evolvepreneur A.I. Advantage.' His podcast features enlightening discussions that promote the democratisation of opportunity for all and demystify AI. These conversations reflect his belief in the power of technology to foster inclusive growth and understanding.

A self-described 'Polynerd,' Richard has an insatiable appetite for knowledge across a broad spectrum of subjects. He utilises this diverse knowledge innovatively, advocating for continuous education and growth as essential components of everyone's success journey. His multidisciplinary approach not only enriches his professional endeavours but also serves as an inspiration for others to follow in their paths to success.

**My Season:**

https://evolvepreneur.app/podcast/category/season-seven-richard

I will start this chapter with a confession and introduce you to a word you've probably not come across before.

"My name is Richard Wray....and I am a 'Polynerd'."

Now, you may have come across the term 'Polymath' before. This is loosely defined as someone who has reached an 'expert' level in several useful subjects and can constructively apply that knowledge. Leonardo Da Vinci, Nikola Tesla, Maria Montessori....Stephen Fry all fall into this category. Some definitions include an average IQ level of 196.

Let me assure you: this is not me.

No, I am a proud Polynerd. By my definition, someone who knows lots of stuff about mainly pointless subjects but can somehow use that mainly pointless stuff in constructive ways. I am very nerdy about many topics and can string a sentence together.

I'll add that I was diagnosed with ADHD at the age of 48. The positives are my ability to hyperfocus on things, learn very quickly (sometimes) and see connections that many others don't. The negatives being...what were we talking about again?

I tell you this to give context about the rest of this chapter. Some references may seem obscure, but trust me...it will all connect.

I've been embracing technology since I was very young. My parents tell a story of when they bought their first VCR. Back then, setting up one of these miracles of technology was not a simple task. Tempers were getting frayed around 1:30 am (the time gets later depending on various factors). Woken by the heated conversation, I wandered downstairs (favorite teddy in hand), looked at the VCR, flicked some switches and had it up and running in about five minutes. Stunned disbelief on their faces.

I couldn't tie my shoelaces, but I could do that!

Look up 'Dilbert – The Knack' for an expanded explanation of this ability. It does not come without downsides.

The one other skill I have developed over the years is to take complex concepts about technology and make them easier to understand.

Right now, I am deeply involved in the field of Artificial Intelligence, or AI for short. In my humble opinion, it is by far and away the biggest game-changing technology in decades, maybe ever. There is so much potential. It is at the same level as The Printing Press, Steam Engine and The Internet. There won't be anyone reading this who hasn't used AI (no, it didn't all start with ChatGPT in November 2022) or whose life won't be affected going forward.

In addition to consulting on AI's uses, I host a podcast called 'The Evolverpreneur A.I. Advantage Show' where I interview experts in their field, run live interactive events and create 'How To' videos through my digital doppelganger 'Pix'*.

https://aiadvantage.show/podcast/theshow

*I am completely unaware of who Max Headroom is and have never heard of him, him, him...

In the podcast, I focus on real-world uses of AI by everyday people whenever possible. Don't get me wrong, I'll happily interview the biggest brains out there, but that's not what I'm about. I want everyone to be able to benefit from AI, try and make sure it is used ethically and dispel the fears and myths that swirl around this topic like killer Sentinel machines around the few remaining humans in The Matrix movies.

*Morpheus – 'A Sentinel for every Zion man, woman, and child. That sounds \*exactly\* like the thinking of a machine to me.'*
—The Matrix Reloaded, 2003

Why did I make that odd reference, especially when this chapter is called 'Don't Mention The Matrix'?

I want you to think about how A.I., machine intelligence or technology in general has been portrayed over the years and the subliminal effect it has had on you. Obviously, this is asking for trouble. There are positive examples, but for every Wall-E from Pixar, there is an army of HAL 9000s (2001: A Space Odessey), Skynets, Terminators, Agent Smiths, Ultrons and even a re-invented Chuckie in the 2019 'Child's Play' remake (voiced by Star Wars' Mark Hamill – be aware of it...don't watch it!).

Society has been conditioned to fear technology, which is being played around A.I. at an elevated level.

*Dr. Ian Malcom – 'Your scientists were so preoccupied with whether or not they could that they didn't stop to think if they should'*
—Jurassic Park, 1993

This isn't necessarily a new thing. There are plenty of historical examples of technology being portrayed as negatively affecting people's lives (at least initially). This feels different though; I'm seeing new patterns.

Let me explain. The subtitle to this chapter is 'The Democratisation Of Paranoia and Opportunity'. I'm going to break this down into two parts. I'll start with 'The Democratisation Of Paranoia'.

*Mary Shelley - "Nothing is so painful to the human mind as a great and sudden change."*
—Frankenstein, 1818

There have always been parts of society that are rarely impacted in a negative way by new technology. Usually, it is the blue-collar workers that feel it. History shows that trying to stop the tide of progress is rarely successful.

A case in point is the story of John Henry. It is a simple tale of a skilled worker who took on a machine designed to do his job. He beat the machine but made such an effort that he died of a heart attack. There was a real John Henry, but the story has become part of American folklore, featured in multiple movies, and he is seen as a hero.

*Anonymous – 'John Henry beat that steam drill down.*
*But he hammered his poor heart to death, Lord, Lord,*
*He hammered his poor heart to death.'*

I see him as less of a hero and more of a cautionary tale. The machine would be able to do the same quality of work the following day. Even if he had survived, I doubt John Henry could perform at the same level repeatedly. Remember, he was the best! The machine could be mass produced. He could not.

Ego, fear, stupidity or maybe a combination of all three, whatever drove him, is something you should not replicate. Pick your battles.

This isn't me attacking the working man. I grew up in a small mining town in England (my father was a miner), and I saw the devastation caused when the mines closed. The resultant drug problem became so bad that a 2002 report stated heroin directly affected one in three people living in the area.

https://www.theguardian.com/society/2002/oct/18/drugsandalcohol.politics
http://news.bbc.co.uk/2/hi/uk_news/england/2339141.stm

*Kyle Reece – 'We were that close to going out forever...'*
—Terminator, 1984

Thankfully, my hometown fought back. It took a while, but it is now thriving again and is popular with commuters. Too bad the government didn't think about this when they closed the mines.

*President Thomas Whitmore – '"We will not go quietly into the night!" We will not vanish without a fight! We're going to live on!'*
—Independence Day (ID4), 1996

I am saying that massive change, be it technological or political, always has a massive impact, but it is usually the blue-collar workers who are hit. A.I. is different.

For maybe the first time, the parts of society that believe they are untouchable are experiencing the same pang of paranoia, that bead of sweat running down the side of their temple that the average working man and family have experienced over the centuries.

Doctors, lawyers, engineers; any highly skilled worker. They are starting to feel it.

When a free resource can craft a perfect answer in seconds from an almost impossibly large database of information, why would anyone pay for the same information? It goes beyond this, though. There are already examples of A.I. detecting breast cancer at a 20% more accurate rate than the standard double reading by two radiologists. If your life or the life of your loved ones depended on it, which option would you choose?

*Sarah Connor - Watching John with the machine, it was suddenly so clear. The terminator would never stop. It would never leave him, and it would never hurt him, never shout at him, or get drunk and hit him, or say it was too busy to spend time with him. It would always be there. And it would die to protect him. Of all the would-be fathers who came and went over the years, this thing, this machine, was the only one who measured up. In an insane world, it was the sanest choice.*
—Terminator 2, 1991

The same concepts can be applied to anything you can think of. I do not believe there is a job or field that will not be affected by the use of Artificial Intelligence. 'A computer will never do my job' will doubtless be one of the statements you have heard at some point. You may have even said it yourself. Now, talk to artists and ask them about Midjourney or DALL-E3 and see how they feel.

This is the democratisation of paranoia!

So what will we do about it, and how is A.I. also 'Democratising Opportunity'?

In the 2004 episode of Southpark 'Goobacks', humans come back from the future and work for a fraction of the cost of the town's residents. Not only was this a great episode, it also birthed a meme.

*Stan – 'They took our jobs!'*
—South Park – Goobacks, 2004

[Small spoilers ahead...give me a break...the episode is nearly 20 years old!!!]

The one solution that the townsfolk came up with that started to work was to improve the present so the future would be, too. The action meant that future humans did not need to travel back in time. Being South Park though, this couldn't last.

I hear a variation of the line 'they took our jobs' (or 'Dey tok yer jobs! Dey tk yer jabbs! Derrker derrrd!' if you want to pronounce it correctly) about A.I. regularly. Whenever the topic of A.I. comes up, one of three items is usually in the conversation somewhere:

- It will take our jobs
- The Terminator
- The Matrix (there I go again mentioning it – sorry)

You may have your own list, but none of this is positive, and as mentioned earlier, all forms of the media make it worse, with lies, half-truths and loaded propaganda being liberally spread.

*Freya - 'Nothing travels faster than light, except gossip.'*
—Matrix Resurrections, 2021

Let's start to get positive. Think about how new technology has been adopted previously. Take my parent's VCR story. The new generation adopted technology without even thinking. There were no barriers in my mind. I just did it! Each new technology becomes a dark art that needs magical incantations with an 'I.T. Wizard' to cast them.

(IF YOU TAKE AWAY ONLY ONE THING FROM READING THIS, MAKE IT THE NEXT LINES!!!!)

Previously, we had to tell a computer how to perform a task.

Here is the massive change. With A.I., we tell the computer what we want!

Lets use the ubiquitous ChatGPT as an example. It primarily works around users writing 'Prompts'—simple conversational instructions to tell it what you want. ChatGPT even refers to it as a 'Chat' (I suppose the clue is in the name). Some professionals focus on creating these prompts.

They are called 'Prompt Engineers' (this does not mean they are engineers who turn up on time...sorry...I couldn't resist). Prompt engineers know how to design the prompt to get the best results, and they can be very complicated. This is great, but I have a theory. I believe that life skills, understanding of topics and the ability to express yourself is something you continue to develop as you age.

By getting past any fears you may have and just trying to use it, you will be amazed at how un-technical it is and how your knowledge of the world and ability to form a coherent sentence produces great results. Think of it like reading a paper map. There is a whole generation that only knows how to use GPS. Those old skills could save your life one day.

To start with, just try the free version of ChatGPT (if it is still available). You won't break it, it won't hack into your bank account, and you won't set off the terminators. More importantly, it won't judge you or call you stupid.

### Have a chat with ChatGPT!

Try asking it to explain something you find difficult in the style of personality you like. Maybe give it a list of ingredients and ask it what you could cook. If you don't like the results, edit the prompt to be clearer about what you want. Use those hard-earned skills; they are coming back into fashion.

You can ask it to write a draft email to someone, maybe in the style of someone you admire.

### Here is a simple example.

Write a very short draft email asking for a discount at a hotel because the last time I stayed there, they lost my luggage.

Subject: Request for Discount Due to Previous Luggage Incident

Dear [Hotel Manager's Name],

I hope this email finds you well. I wanted to reach out to you regarding my previous stay at [Hotel Name] on [Dates of Previous Stay]. While I have always enjoyed my visits to your establishment, I encountered a significant issue during my last stay.

Regrettably, my luggage was misplaced during my stay, causing me a great deal of inconvenience and stress. Your staff worked diligently to resolve the matter, and I appreciate their efforts in assisting me to recover my belongings.

As a loyal guest of [Hotel Name], I was hoping to discuss the possibility of a discount on my next visit as a gesture of goodwill for the inconvenience I experienced. I understand that such situations can be challenging, and I value the commitment of [Hotel Name] to customer satisfaction.

I look forward to your response and hope we can make a mutually agreeable arrangement. Thank you for your attention to this matter.

Yours sincerely,

[Your Name] [Your Contact Information]

Top of Form

That took about 15 seconds, was professional and removed all negative emotion. How long would you have taken to write something like this?

What is this doing? When you get comfortable using the system (this will be fast, I promise), you'll see that those jobs you find difficult or boring can be taken away. It is done so much more quickly by the A.I., leaving you to focus on what is important.

Now, let's have some fun with it. I'll edit the prompt to ask for the response 'in the style of Sean Connery as James Bond while being chased by Russian spies. Make it sound like Sean Connery speaks with phonetic spellings.'

I'm sure you will hear his voice in your head reading the result.

Subject: Urgnt Requezt: Reqest for Discaunt

Deer Esteemed Hotel Management,

I trust this communicaesheun findz yoo in good 'ealth. Ah, the memo'ries of ma last stay at yer establishment still linger in me mind. I couldn't 'elp but remaark on the unique adventshure I 'ad, akin to one of me escapades as James Bond, wit' Russhian spies hot on me trail.

Durin' ma stay, ye seem to 'ave misplaced me luggage, causin' me great inconveenience and disruptshun to ma shapely travel plans. As a loy'al patron of yer fine establisshment, I felt compell'd to bring this matter to yer attenshun.

I kindly request that ye consider providin' me with a discownt on me nex' stay as a gesture of goodwill and as a tokeen of yer commitmint to ensurin' the comfort and satisfacshun of yer esteemed guests. A discownt would 'elp soothe the memory of the past inconveenience and inspire me to return to yer 'otel once more.

I look forrward to yer favourable respohnse and the opportoonity to contiinue enjoyin' the 'ospitality of yer fine establishmint. Please do let me know how ye inten' to adddress this matter.

Yours shincerely,

Sean Connery

'Shincerely' indeed!

Now lets take this to a higher level. You have a great idea. You have come up with a design for a new toothbrush that is 20% more efficient but don't have a clue how to write a business plan to manufacture it.

**Type this into ChatGPT**

I have created a new toothbrush design that is 20% more efficient. Write a business plan to manufacture it.

## Business Plan: Manufacturing and Marketing of the Innovative Toothbrush

### Table of Contents

- Executive Summary
- Company Overview
- Product Description
- Market Analysis
- Competitive Analysis
- Marketing and Sales Strategy
- Operations and Manufacturing
- Financial Projections
- Risk Assessment
- Conclusion

I've removed the actual plan it produced. If you try this you will see how detailed it is. Yet again, in mere seconds, you have a detailed piece of work to begin to personalize.

Maybe this was the one step holding you back from progressing. Maybe English isn't your first language and you find communicating difficult. It doesn't matter. A.I. can enhance and augment your existing skills to make your unique vision a reality. The opportunity that you could never fulfil is now suddenly within reach.

Smith - Lies, lies and more lies.

The Analyst - Smith?

*Smith - What has the world come to when you can't even trust a program?*
—Matrix Resurrections, 2021

One word of caution. All A.I. systems have been known to hallucinate. Check it and use any output as a guide, but always put your own personal spin on it.

These examples have all been text-based. Let's get visual!

I asked ChatGPT's art-creating cousin DALL-E 3:

"Create a logo for a new business making toothbrushes that are 20% better than anyone else's."

Richard Wray - Don't Mention The Matrix

In another tool, I asked, 'Create a promo video for my toothbrushes that are 20% better than anyone else's.'

You can see the results here:

https://evolvepreneursecrets.show/s/toothbrush

I've not even mentioned how you can give ChatGPT different roles like 'accountant', 'marketing head', 'sales lead' and even get them talking to you and each other about how to approach a customer.

See some great examples of this on the Evolvepreneur A.I. Advantage website:

https://aiadvantage.show/podcast/theshow

https://aiadvantage.show/podcast/episode/ais003-001-chatgpt-for-work-life-balance

https://aiadvantage.show/podcast/episode/ais03-ep002-chatgpt-teams

Trinity - What's he doing?

Morpheus - He's beginning to believe.
—The Matrix, 1997

I hope these examples have shown you that A.I. is not to be feared and can be used to give you opportunities that you never thought were possible.

Don't be John Henry and work yourself to death trying to beat the machine.

A.I. won't take your job, but someone using A.I. may do.

A.I. can be a 'Fountain Of Youth' that can increase your output to levels higher than you have ever achieved while spending less time doing it!

You may not even want the job you have once you've tried A.I.

This is 'Opportunity Democratized', without the need for deep pockets or expensive education.

Be Neo from The Matrix. Lose your fear, embrace what is possible and become your true self.

*Just don't mention The Matrix.*
*Neo - Whoa.*
*Neo - I know kung fu.*
—The Matrix, 1997

Connect with me

*https://evolvepreneur.app/s/richardwray*

Chapter 4

# GET MORE PODCAST GUEST INVITATIONS WITH THESE 5 STRATEGIES

**Christine Campbell Rapin**

## About Christine Campbell Rapin

Christine Campbell Rapin is the CEO and owner of CLEAR Acceleration Inc. She is an energetic, tell-it-like-it-is advisor, mentor, consultant and speaker with more than 25 years' experience in marketing, sales and operations working with start-ups to the biggest companies on the planet. To date, she has worked with more than 400 businesses from around the world and across industries to create a combined revenue more than one billion dollars.

She is a sought-after mentor because of her expertise, track record and capabilities to serve as a thinking partner and sounding board to fellow business owners on their journey to creating highly profitable multiple six figure businesses that make a positive impact in the world.

Service-based clients from around the world choose to work with Christine because they seek a seasoned business professional to help guide them to create a consistent client growth engine that supports both top-line and bottom-line revenue growth without working 24/7 or rely on complicated tech and big marketing budgets to scale successfully. They are ready to accelerate their client growth and highly value a thinking partner to pull all the pieces together to create predictable results with less time, effort and money.

Christine is a 2x international best-selling author, has a Bachelor of Commerce and an MBA in International Business from a top 100 school globally, lives in Canada and is married with 2 bonus daughters.

### My Seasons:

https://evolvepreneur.app/podcast/category/season-three-christine
https://evolvepreneur.app/podcast/category/season-five-christine

To have consistent client growth every business owner needs to understand that their business will be built on strangers who become buyers. Therefore, getting in front of more people, more ways, more often and being able to identify the potential buyer for your business are key actions that will fuel future client growth.

There are many ways to expand your audience of potential buyers, however, the 2 most common are:
1. Build your own ecosystem
2. Leverage someone else's ecosystem

While a mix of both strategies deliver the best long-term new client growth results, leveraging someone else's eco-system can be an attractive path to results because it can save time, money and resources when done effectively.

In this chapter, I'm going to talk about podcast guesting which is one of the fastest growing strategies business owners are using to leverage someone else's eco-system to attract new clients.

I'll be sharing five key strategies that when implemented, can lead to more invitations for podcast guest interviews and by being a a great podcast guest interviewee who delivers value to the host's established audience, you can potentially attract more buyers for your business.

Before we jump in to the five strategies, we first need to understand that not all audience members will become buyers.

Buyers, who make up just 3% of the marketplace at any given time, all share 3 key characteristics:
1. They are problem aware.
2. They are actively seeking a solution to resolve the problem.
3. They view resolving the problem as a priority and are open to external support in achieving the result because they know their current strategy is not leading to the desired results.

To accelerate client growth and identify your potential buyers in someone else's eco-system, we need to curate effective marketing strategies that establish as quickly as possible, the all-important "know, like and trust" factors and position our business as the must-hire choice to achieving the results the potential buyer desires.

Buyers begin their purchasing journey through a process which Google has termed the "Zero Moment of Truth" - that pivotal moment when a buyer starts researching the available options in the marketplace with the intent to purchase. Research frequently involves a multi-step, multi-touchpoint experience.

This journey is known as the 7-11-4 phenomenon. Buyers on average spend 7 hours researching a product or service; will engage with 11 touch points and do so in 4 different locations before making a purchase decision.

The potential buyer is actively seeking to determine if the business owner is credible by asking what does the business stand for? Do they walk their talk? And does the potential buyer feel there is alignment between the way the business owner operates with their personal values? They also assessing whether a particular product or service is the best option to help them reach their desired results.

What is important for potential buyers throughout this evaluation journey is that they encounter a well-rounded picture including diverse perspectives vs a one-sided story which can come across as inauthentic and untrustworthy.

In today's digital era, one of the ways buyers are evaluating the zero moment of truth is by listening to podcasts because podcast hosts and guests are increasingly seen as thought leaders and subject matter experts. Potentials buyers value their opinions when looking for recommendations to solve specific problems.

Recently, Demand Sage reported that on average in the USA, 41% of all podcast listeners listen to their favorite shows every month and 28% listen weekly and consume 11 episodes on average. (*https://www.demandsage.com/podcast-statistics*)

Through a podcast guest strategy, not only can you access established, highly targeted audiences of potential buyers in a short period of time, you can also accelerate the potential buyer's journey by borrowing trust simply by sharing a host's platform and host's credibility.

However, as a podcast host who interviewed hundreds of guests both on my own top rated marketing podcast: Amplify Your Marketing Message with Christine Campbell Rapin (*http://www.christinecampbellrapin.com/*

*podcast*) as well as being a guest host on Evolvepreneur After Hours Podcast (*https://evolvepreneur.app/podcast/afterhours*), I can tell you that most business owners are doing a terrible job at effectively leveraging one of the best strategies to grow your audience and attract potential buyers.

I'm going to take you behind the scenes from a host's perspective and share my top five strategies that will help you get invited as a guest onto more podcasts.

In addition, by adopting these strategies, you will be able to maximize podcast guest opportunities which will lead to strong return on investment for your time spent building a podcast guest strategy to attract new clients.

To begin, we need to recognize that podcasting as a whole is about partnership; either a partnership between the host and the audience, or a partnership between the host, the guest being interviewed and the audience. By approaching podcasting with a mindset to proactively seek out mutual benefits, will immediately separate yourself from other podcast guests on this fast-growing media platform.

**The first strategy to adopt is to recognize that podcast guesting as a strategy is not all about you, rather podcasting is an opportunity for mutual benefit.**

With that in mind, please stop pitching your guest appearance for the sole purpose of promoting your own agenda including promoting your programs and services, your book, and your story etc. without regard for the what the host is seeking to create in terms of value for their audience with their podcast.

Individuals are invited to speak on a host's podcast eco-system only when the guest pitch clearly demonstrates how an interview with a potential guest will serve and support the audience that the host has created.

To stand out from the podcast guest applications received, show a host that you've intentionally chosen to apply to be our guest specifically because you've listened to the podcast and are actively pursuing a collaboration with a specific goal in mind that benefits us both.

Take the time to research the host, connect and engage on social media and positively review the show prior to applying to be a guest.

Get to know what the show and the host is all about and seek common ground from which to build your guest pitch around.

Determine if you feel our values are in alignment before applying and always remember that the decision to collaborate on an episode means that we are choosing to join forces to create something greater than we could do on our own.

Your number one goal with your guest episode pitch is to capture the curiosity of the show host or production team. If you cannot do this, you will be an immediate "no" and the decision maker will move on to the next application. That is why I highly recommend you customize your guest pitch around a specific topic or perspective that will benefit the audience and the host.

Generic pitches like "I can talk about mindset, entrepreneurship or marketing" which make you sound like a million other guest applicants. Instead, shift your perspective to a unique viewpoint by telling us exactly what you want to talk about in a broad topic like mindset, entrepreneurship or marketing.

A guest podcast appearance is your opportunity to share what your unique perspective is and most importantly, tell us in very clear language why this would matter to the audience and to the host based on your assessment of what would add value. Remember that we are looking for collaborative partners we can have meaningful discussions with, which listeners will want to engage with and feel inspired to share the episode with others.

**The second strategy to implement to improve your odds of receiving a guest invitation, is to approach this opportunity as a collaborative effort with equal give and take.**

Actively think about what you can do as a podcast guest to grow the ripple effect of this joint venture.

Brainstorm prior to submitting your podcast episode pitch on ways we can work together to maximize this shared experience to grow our individual audiences and include recommendations in your guest application.

As hosts, we are hoping that if you are invited to come into our eco-system and be a guest on our podcast that you are going to be a good partner and reflect well upon our decision to collaborate with in front of our audience of buyers.

Several ways to make the most of the opportunity include sharing publicly on your platforms that you've been invited to appear as a valued guest as well as after the episode is released. To really stand out, consider promoting the episode multiple times after the initial release date. Podcasting as a marketing strategy is a long-term tactic, meaning that content created today has a very long shelf life.

People may listen to an episode today that was originally recorded and released years ago. Therefore, make sure the topics you propose in your podcast guest pitch are topics that you want to be known and discovered for over an extended period vs something time sensitive.

Equally important, always direct audience listeners to an evergreen resource in your call to action, such as your website, to connect with you – something that will still exist years from now.

Be sure that your call to action creates true value and solves a big problem quickly to make a positive first impression as doing so will drive curiosity to know more about your programs and services. You want to avoid breaking the trust factor out of the gate with listeners who may have the potential to become buyers by directing them to a lead magnet or page on your website that won't be relevant in a few months' time.

In terms of promoting your collaboration, have a strategy, follow through with the commitment and plan to promote the episode.

Think creatively about how you utilize and create content. This may range from posts on social media (be sure to ask your host how they'd like the show tagged as some may want you to tag them personally, under a business name or a combination), inclusion in your newsletters or blogs and adding the content into your website. All of which have long term SEO value to the host through backlinks.

Lastly, be sure to share the episode with other people in your industry and in groups and communities where you network.

Always include a detailed plan in your podcast guest application showcasing your promotional commitment. This will generate interest with many hosts, as it shows you have thought about how we mutually can benefit from a potential collaboration.

**The third key strategy to increase the long-term results as a podcast guest is to focus on building a long-term relationship with the host.**

Avoid approaching your podcast guest strategy as a one-time exchange. Doing so can minimize your overall long-term impact to fuel client growth.

Relationships begin well before we receive your pitch and can last for many years after an episode is recorded and released. Therefore, network proactively with host before, during and after being invited on as a podcast guest.

Think about how you can add value to the host's network. Support their business goals and give generously out of the gate by thinking proactively about who you can recommend as other potential guests or as collaborative partners to the host. Take time to give the host a shout out on your platforms and shine light on the host's business and the podcast itself.

By focusing on building a long term mutually beneficial partnership, you open the door to creating mutual wins well beyond the single podcast episode. In fact, many lucrative revenue opportunities can be created from a solid first collaboration including: revenue sharing, joint ventures, co-creation of content and referrals to name a few.

Explore with your host the possibilities to create ripples together both in the short and long term. Both of your businesses will evolve and by staying connected, you may be able to open doors for each other that lead to client growth and additional opportunities for collaboration.

**The fourth strategy to becoming a sought-after podcast guests where you effectively use someone else's eco-system to attract new clients is by having a strongly held opinion and the ability to communicate clearly the lens in which you view the world.**

The key to success as a podcast guest is to drop the jargon that makes you sound like everyone else. Think proactively about how your unique viewpoint can benefit the audience to act, see a different perspective or reinforce their own beliefs.

Think about what will spark the audience's curiosity to listen to the episode and want to connect with you further after listening to this episode to explore your programs and services.

Know confidently what you stand for, the value you want to bring to the conversation and articulate this in your podcast episode pitch. As hosts, we are looking for thought leaders who walk their talk, boldly state their values, opinions and perspectives and guests that will bring a unique voice to the overall podcast.

**The fifth and final strategy to become podcast guest that effectively uses this marketing strategy to attract an audience of buyers is to be professional.**

Approaching podcast guesting professionally should be a given, however experience tells me that this unfortunately is often overlooked.

Listen here: www.evolvepreneursecrets.show

At a minimum, you should show up on time, in the right location, stick to the talking points agreed and follow through on the promotional plan to maximize the episode reach. Guests should have a professional background with good lighting and high-quality sound. Remember for the audience of listeners, this may be their first impression of you, and you want it to be a positive one.

How you show up will set the tone for future interactions and this episode may be the zero moment of truth for your next client. Be intentional with your brand positioning and use this podcast guest collaboration to reinforce your position as a thought leader that adds value.

Demonstrate that you can be trusted to help potential buyers solve their problems and invite them to choose you as the must hire choice when the time is right to purchase.

Podcast guesting can be a fun and effective way to access new audiences and attract potential buyers by leveraging someone else's eco-system.

The real Return on Investment (ROI) of these five key strategies is when you are viewed as a sought-after guest that consistently attracts new clients through podcast guest appearances.

To recap the five strategies that help you get booked on more podcasts:
1. Focus on podcast guesting as a win-win strategy to reach new audiences of potential buyers.
2. Focus on making your podcast guest appearance a collaborative marketing strategy.
3. Focus on building a long-term relationship with the host to maximize your return on investment and create new opportunities beyond the initial podcast episode.
4. Focus on your unique viewpoint and articulate why and how adds value for this specific podcast audience and host.
5. Focus on being professional throughout the experience to position yourself as a thought leader and respected podcast guest collaborative partner. .

As podcasting continues to grow, remember that top shows have lots of choice for guests. In fact, there are more people looking to be guests than hosts looking for guests. Top hosts are looking for guest collaborators that will bring unique viewpoints that will create highly valued content to drive engagement and downloads.

As a podcast guest remember that every step in the process matters.

Show up at every step with your best foot forward and invest in creating a quality podcast guest application and experience because both hosts and audience members are looking for guests who bring their A-game and deliver valued results. Your next podcast guest appearance just may be the zero moment of truth for you for your next client.

Business growth can be elegantly simple, it is not however, effortless.

If you are a business owner struggling to create a client growth engine and don't know how to identify and attract buyers with effective marketing messaging that nurtures and moves general audience members into the buying cycle with high conversion rates, then I invite you to explore the Business Scale Accelerator Mentorship Program. In this high-touch program, we help business owners get clarity and establish themselves as the must hire in order to see consistent results.

Visit *http://www.christinecampbellrapin.com* to explore the program options.

**Connect with me**

*https://evolvepreneur.app/s/christine*

Chapter 5

# LAYING BRICKS: BUILDING A BUSINESS FOUNDATION

**David Kitchen**

## About David Kitchen

Coach Kitch is the Founder and President of Edge Leadership Academy. He is a former Division 1 Coach, and a PhD Candidate with a master's degree in sport psychology, who has a decade of experience building leaders, culture, and mindset at the highest levels of sports and business. He is the author of The Pyramid: A System for Building Tomorrow's Leaders Today, and The Scoreboard: A Self-Audit System to Help You Build the Life You Want. As an award-winning speaker, consultant, and coach, Coach Kitch is trusted by 100+ CEO's, coaches, and high performers to help them lead and win in business, athletics, and life.

Listen here: www.evolvepreneursecrets.show

## Built Not Born: My Leadership Philosophy

### Introduction

When I think about my life's journey, I'm reminded that the path to leadership is neither straight nor easy. Many see leadership as a destination, a title to be attained, or goosebumps moments delivered in front of a crowd. But my experiences have taught me otherwise; leadership is a continuous journey of skill building, one that I have learned through experiences, mentorship, and research and now look to teach to others.

### The Origin Story

Let's rewind the tape a bit and start from the beginning. I was born into a single-parent household, a setting that many would consider less than ideal for nurturing a future leader. Resources were limited, and luxuries were few and far between. But what I had in abundance was love and a set of core values that were instilled in me from a young age.

My mother was my first role model; the epitome of resilience and determination. She worked multiple jobs to make ends meet, but always found time to teach me life's essential lessons. She was my first leadership coach, instilling in me values like integrity, humility, and a relentless work ethic. It was from her that I learned the foundational lesson that leadership starts at home, long before one steps into the corporate world.

### The Misconception of Born Leaders

As I grew older and stepped into various leadership roles, I found myself confronting the deeply ingrained notion that leaders are born. I couldn't disagree more. I am a living testament to the contrary. Leaders are built, not born.

The 'born leader' stereotype is not just misleading; it's dangerous. It perpetuates a kind of elitism that suggests leadership is an exclusive club, open only to those with the 'right' qualities, background, or even genetics. I've spent a significant part of my professional life challenging this misconception, both in my practices and my writings.

If leadership were an inherited trait, then training and development would be moot points. But that's far from the truth. Leadership is a skill, one that can be honed through experience, learning, and conscious effort.

## Lead Yourself First

### The Value of Character: More Than Just a Buzzword

The term "character" is often tossed around casually, almost becoming a buzzword in many corporate settings. But for me, character isn't just a term; it's the bedrock upon which my entire leadership philosophy is built.

### Vision: The North Star

Having a vision is like having a North Star; it provides direction and purpose. It's important to recognize that as a leader, your personal vision, mission, and values are going to be reflected in your business. They don't need to be identical, but everything you touch will have your signature on it. Define who you are as a person first, and then intertwine your signature into your business vision, mission, and values.

Your personal vision is what you ultimately want for yourself. This is the big picture, but it should be somewhat tangible. For example, I want to leave a legacy for my family to be proud of. This is the ultimate goal for me as a man and stems from my own personal beliefs. This vision is in the back of my mind at all times and influences all the decisions I make.

By having a personal vision statement that guides you, you can now lead authentically. As Simon Sinek said, "people don't buy products, they buy people."

### Mission: The How-To Manual

While a vision outlines the 'what' and 'why,' a mission focuses on the 'how.' It's crucial to ensure that your mission aligns seamlessly with your vision. This alignment turns your vision from a lofty ideal into a practical, achievable goal. It's the roadmap that turns your leadership journey from a meandering walk in the forest into a focused journey to the peak. In simpler terms, what will you do on a daily basis that if done consistently, will achieve the vision?

The mission you choose is the how-to manual of executing your vision. How will you accomplish what you envision? For me, I will inspire greatness in those around me. The easiest way to begin this is by utilizing your vision statement from above. Again, using my own example, I will leave a legacy for my family to be proud of by inspiring greatness in those around me. The impact I have will lead to the legacy I leave.

### Values: Your Insurance Policy

Values are the foundation of your identity. When everything else is stripped away, what do you stand for? Better yet, what do you *fight for*? For the sake of simplicity, I'd suggest writing a list of no more than 20 words and phrases that mean a lot to you. Once you've compiled your list, find the common threads and use 3-5 of those phrases or words as your values. Again, it's easiest to put it into sentence form. For example, I am driven, honest, caring, and committed to growth.

### Putting it Together

When you combine your vision, mission, and values you will be left with three powerful sentences that should sum up your character. Think about it as the opening paragraph of your eulogy if you wrote it yourself. *Example: I left a legacy for my family to be proud of. I inspired greatness in those around me. I was driven, honest, caring, and committed to growth.*

### Putting Your Vision to Work

As a leader, you will face difficult decisions, distractions, temptations, and opportunities to stray from your path. When you have a clear understanding of your vision, your mission, and your values, decisions begin to make themselves. Lean on your VMV statement from above to make daily decisions easy. I use this for business opportunities, partnerships, and even simple things such as deciding whether or not to watch that one extra episode of Netflix. For every decision, I ask myself 3 questions:

1. Does it bring me closer to my vision?
2. Does this allow me the opportunity to fulfill my mission?
3. Do I get to exercise the values I believe in?

Put simply, if I don't answer "yes" to all 3 questions, there's a 90% chance I won't do it. However, if for some reason I'm still debating it, I take the test a step further. I get clear on what exactly I'd be sacrificing (vision, mission, or values), *why* the ends may justify the means, and finally I decide exactly how long I'm willing to tolerate this disconnect from my VMV. If I choose to proceed,

I outline an exact outcome that I want to achieve and an expiration date on the disconnect. If I haven't achieved the outcome by the time the expiration date comes, I cut my losses and end the project regardless of the sacrifice. Nothing is worth straying from your vision, mission, and values indefinitely.

## The Moral Compass

The importance of a strong moral compass in leadership cannot be overstated. It's the ethical framework that guides all our actions, decisions, and interactions. I've found that leaders with a strong moral compass not only attract like-minded individuals but also cultivate a culture of integrity within their organization. This involves more than just following rules; it's about creating an environment where doing the right thing is the norm. Real-life examples can serve as powerful lessons. Doing the right thing because it's the right thing as a leader tells your team what matters in your company. What you tolerate is what will continue, and what you model is what will be reflected. I've always believed that your true character is revealed not in your actions on a stage, but in those quiet moments when you're faced with tough choices. How you react in those instances defines you as a leader.

Although your character is reflected far beyond your business, it also shows up as in key places inside your business. The most glaring places that your character is on display is your habits, your social interactions, your self-regulatory behaviors, and your mindset.

Your habits directly reflect your character for a few reasons. First, time is your most valuable resource, so how you spend it tells your team everything they need to know about you. Second, where you deploy your energy consistently reflects what's important to you. As a leader, it is key to have habits that reflect the pursuit of the vision you've set forth.

Social interactions and your social circle are another key indicator of your character. Leaders should be hyper-aware of the way they treat people. What you model is what will continue. Ask yourself; how do you treat people when you're in a good mood, bad mood, or when you're interacting with those who can do nothing for you? This test can also be useful when identifying and interviewing potential hires, business partners, or clients. I'm always watching how people treat the Uber driver, the doorman, and the waiter. I'm also listening closely to how they discuss people who are not in the room. These small instances are a powerful glimpse into someone's character.

Your social circle falls under the same scrutiny as your social interactions. We know all the clichés about becoming the sum of the 5 people you spend the most time with, and I will be the first to defend these clichés. The most successful leaders I've been around are intentional and meticulous about how they curate their social circle. When you're making decisions that influence people's lives and impact your business, it's important to moderate who has access to and influence on you.

It's no secret that your team is looking to you in times of adversity, failures, and success. During these times, your team wants to know if you can be swayed by the emotion of the moment. The key to handling these moments with grace and poise is to understand that between the stimulus and your response (or reaction) is a gap. Great leaders are experts at navigating this gap and mitigating the emotions to make a rational and reasoned decision.

Lastly, your mindset is a key indicator of your character. Arrogant, fearful, and ineffective leaders operate under a fixed mindset. They live by "that's the way we've always done it". Effective leaders operate from a place of vision, mission, and value alignment. In other words, they are flexible in the approach, but disciplined in the desired outcome.

Put simply, your actions as a leader set the tone for your team; make sure you're someone worth following that's going somewhere worth going.

## Crafting a Shared Vision

Once you've gotten clear on your personal vision, it's important to intertwine it with your business vision. A business vision is not something to be hoarded or kept under lock and key; it's something to be shared with your team, your stakeholders, and anyone else who is a part of your journey. I make it a point to involve my team in the vision-crafting process. When everyone has a stake in the vision, it transforms from being 'my vision' to 'our vision,' and that collective ownership is incredibly empowering.

## The Practical Facets of Leadership

### Building a Team: More Than Just Skill Sets

When I speak of team building, I'm not just talking about hiring the right skills. Soft skills are often overlooked but are crucial for a harmonious work environment. Emotional intelligence, effective communication, and conflict resolution skills are just as important as technical prowess. Investing in training programs that hone these soft skills can be invaluable for fostering a strong, cohesive team.

## The 'Right Fit'

One phrase you'll often hear in the corporate world is the 'right fit.' But what does that really mean? For me, the right fit is someone whose values align with the organization's, whose vision resonates with the team's, and whose character stands up to scrutiny.

## The Interview Process: Beyond the Obvious

When it comes to hiring, I give a lot of weight to an individual's character. For me, a resume can showcase your skills and experiences, but it's character that reveals your potential. When I conduct interviews, I often stray from the traditional script of asking about past experiences and qualifications. Instead, I ask questions that give me insights into the candidate's thought processes, ethical stance, and adaptability. I can teach skills, but I recruit character.

## Mentorship: A Two-Way Street

Mentorship is often viewed as a one-sided relationship where a more experienced individual guides a less experienced one. However, I've found mentorship to be a two-way street, offering rewards for both parties involved. I recall mentoring a young employee who introduced me to new technologies and ways of thinking, enriching my perspective. On the flip side, as a mentee, my mentors have provided invaluable advice that has accelerated my career development. The essence here is that mentorship relationships should be symbiotic, filled with mutual respect and shared learning.

## Becoming a Mentor

As I progressed in my career, I found myself transitioning from the role of a mentee to that of a mentor. This shift wasn't just a milestone but a responsibility. Mentorship is not about creating a mini-me; it's about helping someone discover their own leadership style while imparting the wisdom gained from your own experiences.

I firmly believe in the circle of mentorship, where today's mentees become tomorrow's mentors. This cycle not only ensures the continuity of leadership qualities but also creates a culture of mutual growth and learning. You should always be in both types of relationships. I like to have a mentee who wants to be where I am, and a mentor who is where I want to be.

Listen here: www.evolvepreneursecrets.show

If there's one thing that's constant in life and business, it's change. As leaders, we must not only adapt to change but also continually strive to be better. This philosophy of continuous improvement is not just a business strategy; it's a life mantra. The best way to be ready for that change is to be surrounded by new ideas and tried and true principles.

## Resilience: The Bedrock of Leadership

In my experience, resilience is one of the most critical qualities a leader can possess. The business landscape is filled with challenges, setbacks, and failures. But it's not these obstacles that define us; it's how we navigate them. Resilience is more than just a personal trait—it's a culture that can permeate an entire organization. When team members see their leaders handle challenges as an opportunity and not a threat, it sets a precedent for how they should respond to difficulties as well.

As a leader, fostering resilience involves acknowledging challenges and setbacks as learning opportunities. It means being transparent with your team about challenges while maintaining a firm hold on the vision as the north star. The power of resilience lies in its ability to transform negative experiences into stepping stones for growth. Win or learn. This mindset is not just suggested, but is required for success in the world of entrepreneurship. Your team will be a reflection of your mindset, vision, mission, and values.

In my journey, every failure has been a stepping stone to success. When you shift your perspective in this way, every challenge becomes a lesson, and every obstacle becomes an opportunity for growth. Each failure has been a teacher in its own right, imparting lessons that no success ever could. Whether it was a failed project, a poor hiring decision, or a flawed strategy, each misstep has given me insights that have been instrumental in shaping my leadership style. Failures aren't setbacks; they're setups for comebacks (if you're willing to reflect).

## The Inevitability of Failure: It's Not the End

If you're in a leadership role and haven't faced failure, you're either incredibly lucky or not taking enough risks. Failure is not just a possibility; it's an inevitability. And that's perfectly okay. In many corporate cultures, failure is stigmatized, almost seen as a scarlet letter. This perception needs to change. Failure is not a mark of incompetence; it's a mark of effort, a sign that you're pushing boundaries and stepping out of your comfort zone.

## Measuring Success: Impact Over Numbers

I've always believed that the true measure of success lies in the impact you create. Have you improved lives? Have you solved problems? Have you made things easier, better, more efficient? These questions are as important as any figure on a balance sheet.

Numbers can show trends and offer a snapshot view, but they often lack depth. Qualitative methods like employee surveys, customer interviews, or even casual conversations can provide invaluable insights into the emotional and psychological state of your team and customers. These "soft" metrics are crucial for any leader focused on building a culture rooted in empathy and understanding.

## Looking Ahead: The Future of Leadership

In today's ever-changing landscape, adaptability is more important than ever. It's not just about being flexible as an individual leader; it's also about fostering a culture of adaptability within your team or organization. Encourage open dialogue and be willing to pivot your strategies when necessary. Create an environment where employees are not just allowed but encouraged to bring new ideas to the table. Regular training programs focused on developing adaptive skills can also be highly beneficial.

## Actionable Checklist for Aspiring Leaders

Leadership is not just about theory; it's about practice. To truly develop your leadership skills, you need to take concrete steps. Below is a checklist of actions you can take to pave your path towards effective leadership.

### Character Building

**Self-Assessment**: Take a moment to evaluate your core values. Are they in alignment with your actions?

**Integrity Test:** Think of a situation where it was difficult to do the right thing. Did you compromise your values?

### Vision Crafting

**Vision Statement**: Write down a vision statement for your leadership journey. Make it as detailed as possible.

**Share Your Vision:** Share this vision with someone you trust and ask for feedback.

**Vision Check**: Periodically review your vision and adjust as necessary.

## Team Building

**Skill Inventory:** Make a list of the skills you possess and the skills you lack but need.

**Team Assessment**: Evaluate your team's skills and character. Do they align with your vision?

**Hiring Practices:** Next time you're involved in hiring, incorporate character assessment into the process.

## Mentorship

**Find a Mentor**: Seek out someone whose leadership style you admire and ask them for guidance.

**Be a Mentor:** Offer to guide someone who is earlier in their leadership journey.

**Mentorship Review**: Periodically review what you've learned and imparted in your mentor-mentee relationships.

## Continuous Learning

**Education Plan**: Develop a plan for your ongoing education. This could include books, courses, or workshops.

**Skill Update**: Learn something new every quarter. It doesn't have to be a big skill; even a small one counts.

**Feedback Loop**: Regularly ask for feedback and act on it.

## Failure and Success Metrics

**Failure Journal:** Keep a journal of your failures and the lessons each one taught you.

**Success Metrics**: Define what success means to you, beyond financial metrics.

**Impact Measurement:** Periodically assess the impact you're making. Is it aligned with your vision?

By following this checklist, you can take actionable steps towards becoming a more effective leader. Remember, leadership is not a destination but a journey of continuous growth and learning.

## Summary

In this chapter, I've aimed to share my perspectives on building a solid foundation for both leadership and business. I began by introducing the concept that leadership isn't a destination but a journey using my own origin story to highlight how my past experiences have shaped my leadership style.

I've discussed the critical role of a moral compass in guiding actions and decisions, emphasizing the importance of aligning this compass with the broader vision and mission of the organization. I've also spoken about the necessity of hiring the right people and fostering a culture of mentorship.

I tackled the often-avoided topic of failure, arguing that it should be viewed as a learning opportunity rather than a stigma. I explored the idea that success shouldn't be measured purely by numbers but should also consider impact and people-centric metrics. I concluded by emphasizing the importance of adaptability, character building, and continuous learning in today's fast-paced world.

The essence of this chapter is that effective leadership and a strong business foundation go hand-in-hand, and one cannot exist without the other. I've shared these insights not as hard-and-fast rules but as foundational bricks that have helped me in my journey so far.

I hope that these insights will serve as useful building blocks for your own leadership journey. I encourage you to keep laying your own bricks as you continue to grow both as a leader and as an individual.

## A Personal Message to Future Leaders

As I sit here reflecting on my journey, the triumphs and the setbacks, the highs and the lows, I'm reminded of the immense responsibility that comes with leadership. It's not just about steering a ship; it's about guiding the people on that ship, ensuring they have the tools, the motivation, and the vision to row together towards a shared horizon.

Leadership is not a title or a position; it's a mindset, a commitment to excellence, not just in yourself but in those around you. It's about laying the bricks of a strong foundation, not just for a successful career but for a fulfilling life.

So, as you turn the pages of this chapter and move on to your own chapters, remember that you're not alone. You're part of a community, a lineage of leaders who have faced challenges, overcome obstacles, and emerged stronger. And just like I had mentors to guide me, you too will find your tribe.

I look forward to hearing your stories, learning from your experiences, and celebrating your successes.

Connect with me

*https://evolvepreneur.app/s/davidkitchen*

Listen to David's Episode

*https://evolvepreneur.app/s/eps06-38*

Listen here: www.evolvepreneursecrets.show

Chapter 6

# PROFITABLE GROWTH IS ACHIEVABLE

**Manny Skevofilax**

## About Manny Skevofilax

Manny Skevofilax is a consultant and speaker that helps his clients successfully navigate the challenges of growing their businesses profitably. Since 2003, Manny helps businesses enhance their results by using his experience in strategic planning, financial statement analysis, operations, organizational development, and team-building. His consulting firm, PORTAL CFO Consulting, Inc., has attracted clients from diverse industries in the United States and abroad.

Listen here: www.evolvepreneursecrets.show

## Introduction: The Cornerstone of Profitable Growth

Hello, I'm Manny Skevofilax, and I'm thrilled to have you here on this journey towards profitable growth. Many businesses strive for growth, but not all growth is profitable — and that's where the key difference lies. Profitable growth is sustainable, strategic, and most importantly, leads to a healthy bottom line. In this chapter, we'll delve into the strategies, insights, and actionable steps that can guide you to achieve this elusive form of growth.

## Understanding Goals and Capabilities: The Starting Point

Before diving headlong into any growth strategy, it's crucial to have a rock-solid understanding of your goals and capabilities. It might sound basic, but you'd be surprised how many businesses miss this foundational step. Assess your business landscape. Know your strengths, understand your weaknesses, and have a crystal-clear vision of what success looks like for you. Only then can you plot a course that leads to true profitable growth.

## Client Relationships: The Backbone of Your Business

Your clients are more than just entries in a ledger. They are the lifeblood of your business and the cornerstone of your growth. You've got to treat these relationships as sacred. Without a strong client base, all your strategies, all your marketing, and all your efforts will fall flat. The question you should be asking is not just how you can gain more clients, but how you can serve them better.

## Project Management: The Balancing Act

You're eager to grow, and it's tempting to bite off more than you can chew. But have caution! Taking on too many projects can be a surefire recipe for disaster. Quality over quantity should be your mantra. The key is to take on projects where you can deliver exceptional value, rather than spreading yourself too thin.

## Effective Communication: The Unsung Hero of Business Operations

In any business, effective communication is the glue that holds everything together. Miscommunications, misunderstandings, and assumptions are often the root cause of project failures, client dissatisfaction, and team discord. The remedy? Clear, concise, and frequent communication. Your team should know what's expected, your clients should be kept in the loop, and you should be the conductor orchestrating this flow of information.

### Financial Planning: Beyond Keeping the Lights On

Talking numbers isn't the most glamorous part of running a business, but it's undoubtedly one of the most crucial. Financial planning goes beyond merely keeping your business afloat; it's about strategic allocation of resources for future growth. Invest in the right technologies, hire the right talent, and most importantly, have a rainy-day fund. Smart financial planning today sets the stage for profitable growth tomorrow.

### Innovation: A Non-Negotiable for Competitive Edge

The business landscape is constantly changing. New technologies, evolving customer expectations, and global challenges mean that standing still is the same as going backward. Innovation isn't a buzzword; it's a business imperative. From process improvements to product enhancements, keep an eye out for opportunities to innovate.

### Team Culture: More Than Just Perks and Benefits

You could have the most innovative products and the most meticulous plans, but if your team isn't onboard, you're sailing a rudderless ship. A motivated, engaged, and skilled team is your biggest asset. Create a culture that values growth, nurtures talent, and rewards initiative. A strong team culture is often the secret sauce in the recipe for long-term, profitable growth.

### Actionable Steps for Achieving Profitable Growth

1. **Conduct a SWOT Analysis**: Allocate time and resources to perform a comprehensive Strengths, Weaknesses, Opportunities, and Threats analysis. Involve your team and consider bringing in an external expert for an unbiased perspective.
2. **Set SMART Goals**: Establish goals that are Specific, Measurable, Achievable, Relevant, and Time-bound. Review these goals quarterly to adjust for any changes in business conditions.
3. **Invest in Client Relationships**: Develop a customer relationship management (CRM) strategy to maintain and enhance relationships with your existing clients.

4. **Prioritise Project Management**: Use project management tools to keep track of timelines, responsibilities, and budgets. Don't hesitate to turn down projects that don't align with your capabilities and goals.
5. **Implement Effective Communication Channels**: Choose the right tools for internal and external communication. Regularly update your team and clients to keep everyone in the loop.
6. **Create a Financial Plan:** Work with your finance team to create a 12-month financial plan. Update this plan as conditions change and new information becomes available.
7. **Cultivate a Culture of Innovation**: Set aside a budget and resources for Research & Development. Create an internal rewards program to encourage innovative ideas from your team.
8. **Build a Strong Team Culture**: Invest in employee development programs and create an environment where feedback is welcomed and acted upon.
9. **Utilise Data Analytics**: Invest in data analytics tools that can help you make sense of business metrics and customer behavior.
10. **Develop a Marketing and Branding Strategy**: Clearly define your brand's voice, look, and feel. Implement a multi-channel marketing strategy that aligns with this brand identity.
11. **Plan for Sustainability**: Review your business operations to identify areas where you can implement more sustainable practices.
12. **Ethical Business Practices**: Create a code of conduct and ethics that every team member understands and agrees to follow.
13. **Prepare for Crisis Management**: Develop a crisis management plan and conduct regular drills with your team.
14. **Focus on Customer Experience**: Implement policies and training programs aimed at improving customer experience at every touchpoint.
15. **Consider Global Expansion**: If applicable, start researching potential markets for global expansion. Use this research to inform your expansion strategy.

## Digital Transformation: More Than a Buzzword

The term 'digital transformation' has been bandied about so much that it's easy to dismiss it as just another business buzzword. However, in an increasingly digital world, the ability to adapt new technologies into your business operations is critical. This doesn't mean blindly adopting every new software or gadget that hits the market. It means carefully evaluating which technologies can add real value to your business. It involves training your team to use these new tools effectively, integrating them into your existing workflows, and continuously monitoring their impact on your business performance.

## The Importance of Work-Life Balance

In the quest for growth, it's easy to overlook the well-being of your most valuable asset—your team. Burnout is a very real issue that can have serious consequences on your business, from decreased productivity to higher turnover rates. Encourage a healthy work-life balance by offering flexible working arrangements, promoting regular breaks, and respecting personal time. A happy, healthy team is far more likely to give their best, and that's a win-win for everyone involved.

The concept of remote work has been around for a while, but recent global events have accelerated its adoption. It's not just a temporary solution but a long-term strategy that offers benefits and challenges. Communication is vital in a remote setup. Use collaborative tools to maintain the same level of interaction you would have in an office. Regular check-ins and video conferences can help maintain team unity. Additionally, setting clear expectations and performance metrics can help maintain productivity levels. Remote work is not a trend; it's an evolution in how we think about work.

## Community Involvement: Beyond the Bottom Line

While the ultimate goal of any business is profitability, it's also important to consider the impact you have on the community around you. Community involvement not only enhances your brand's reputation but can also offer tangible benefits like networking opportunities and increased customer loyalty. Whether it's by sponsoring local events, participating in community service, or running educational workshops, giving back to the community can be a fulfilling experience that pays long-term dividends. The digital landscape is not just changing; it's evolving at a breakneck speed.

Businesses that don't adapt risk becoming obsolete. But let's get one thing straight: digital transformation is not about throwing technology at problems. It's a strategic initiative that requires a deep understanding of your business processes, customer needs, and market dynamics. It's about aligning your business goals with your digital capabilities. You'll need a skilled team to drive this transformation, and it's crucial to get buy-in from the top down. After all, a tool is only as effective as the person wielding it.

Metrics matter, but it's easy to get lost in a sea of numbers. The key is to focus on Key Performance Indicators (KPIs) that are directly aligned with your business goals. It's not about tracking every possible metric but about zeroing in on the ones that provide actionable insights. You may start with broad metrics like revenue and customer acquisition, but as your business grows, your KPIs should become more nuanced.

Perhaps you'll start tracking customer engagement levels, or maybe employee satisfaction becomes a priority. Either way, make sure your KPIs evolve with your business.

## Customer Feedback: A Goldmine of Insights

In today's hyper-connected world, customers aren't shy about sharing their opinions. And that's something every business should take advantage of. Customer feedback, both positive and negative, provides invaluable insights into what you're doing right and where you can improve. Regularly solicit feedback through surveys, reviews, and direct interactions. But collecting feedback is just the first step; acting on it is where the real value lies.

In the age of social media, customer feedback is instantaneous and public. While this can be a double-edged sword, it's also an invaluable resource for continuous improvement. But don't just wait for feedback to come to you; seek it out. Conduct regular customer surveys, monitor online reviews, and even consider setting up a customer advisory board. The more data you collect, the clearer the picture you'll have of what you're doing right and where you need to improve. But remember, data without action is just trivia. Use the insights you gain to drive real change.

Adaptability is not a one-time effort but a continuous process. The business landscape is always changing, and the ability to adapt is what sets successful businesses apart from the ones that get left behind. This is where having a flexible business model comes into play. Can you pivot your services to meet new market demands? Can you adapt your products to cater to a different audience? The more adaptable you are, the more resilient your business will be in the face of challenges.

## Remote Work: The New Normal?

The recent global events have forced many businesses to adopt remote working arrangements, and for many, this change could be permanent. Remote work offers several advantages, including reduced overhead costs and increased access to a wider talent pool. However, it also presents challenges like maintaining team cohesion and ensuring productivity. Effective communication, regular check-ins, and the right collaboration tools are essential for making remote work, work.

Community involvement is not just good PR; it's good business. It's about building lasting relationships that extend beyond the conference room. Whether it's supporting local charities, sponsoring youth programs, or participating in community clean-ups, these activities show that you're a brand that cares. And in today's socially conscious world, this can be a significant differentiator. But don't just do it for the optics; do it because it's the right thing to do. The goodwill you earn will more than make up for the time and resources spent.

## Marketing and Branding: More than Just Buzzwords

Today's marketing goes beyond the traditional 4 Ps—Product, Price, Place, and Promotion. We're now in an era where the consumer wields unprecedented power, thanks to the information at their fingertips. Effective marketing today is about conversations, not just broadcasting messages. It's a two-way street, where you not only speak to your audience but also listen to what they have to say. Utilise tools like social listening to gain insights into consumer sentiment and tailor your strategies accordingly. Remember, your brand is not just your logo or your tagline; it's the entire experience you offer your customers.

## Sustainability: The Future is Green

Sustainability has moved from being a 'nice-to-have' to a 'must-have.' It's no longer sufficient to simply meet legal requirements; you need to go above and beyond. Make sustainability a core part of your business strategy, not just an appendage. It should inform your choices from sourcing materials to waste management. But don't just stop at your operations; consider your entire supply chain. Engage with suppliers who share your commitment to sustainability. The ripple effect can be far-reaching and can enhance your brand value exponentially.

## Business Ethics: The Foundation of Trust

Business ethics go beyond just legal compliance; they're about building a culture of doing the right thing, even when no one is watching. This is something that needs to come from the top. Leadership sets the tone for the entire organisation. Regular training sessions on ethical conduct, transparent grievance mechanisms, and a zero-tolerance policy towards unethical behaviour are essential. Remember, trust is hard to earn but easy to lose. Uphold the highest ethical standards to build a reputation that can withstand any scrutiny.

Listen here: www.evolvepreneursecrets.show

## Talent Management: Your Team, Your Asset

Having a great team is like having a secret weapon. Talent management is not just about hiring the right people but also about retaining them. Continuous training, clear career progression paths, and a positive work environment are all part of effective talent management. Remember, a motivated team is a productive team, and their growth directly correlates with your business growth. Consider investing in team-building activities, mentorship programs, and even mental health support services to create an environment where your employees can thrive.

## E-commerce: The Digital Frontier

E-commerce is not just an additional sales channel; it's the future. With an increasing number of consumers choosing to shop online, having a robust e-commerce strategy is no longer optional. You need to provide a seamless customer experience. Invest in a user-friendly website, secure payment gateways, and efficient logistics to make online shopping a pleasure for your customers. Customer reviews and testimonials can be a powerful tool, so encourage satisfied customers to share their experiences. Invest in employee well-being for a truly unified and motivated team.

## Networking: Your Business Catalyst

Networking doesn't mean handing out business cards at events and hoping for the best. It's about forming meaningful relationships that can provide value in the long term. Whether it's finding a mentor, securing a business partner, or even meeting a future employee, networking can be a game-changer for your business. Attend industry events, join relevant online communities, and don't underestimate the power of a warm introduction. Building a strong network takes time but the rewards are well worth it.

## Time Management: Maximising Every Minute

In business, time is money. Effective time management is not just about working harder but working smarter. Prioritise your tasks, delegate when possible, and don't be afraid to say no when necessary. Utilise tools like project management software to keep track of deadlines and responsibilities. Remember, being busy is not the same as being productive. Be mindful of how you're spending your time and make adjustments as needed to ensure you're focusing on what truly matters.

## Global Reach: Expanding Beyond Borders

In today's interconnected world, the market is not just your local community; it's global. However, global expansion comes with its own set of challenges, from cultural differences to logistical complexities. Do thorough market research and consider partnering with local businesses to better understand the landscape. Adapt your products or services to meet local needs and preferences. Going global is a significant step, but with the right strategy, it can be a game-changer for your business.

## Customer Service: The Unsung Hero

Good customer service can turn a one-time buyer into a lifelong customer. It's not just about resolving issues but exceeding expectations. Train your customer service team to not just answer questions but to anticipate needs. Use customer feedback to continuously improve your service. A satisfied customer is your best marketing tool, so invest in providing an exceptional customer experience.

## Social Media: More than Just Likes and Shares

Social media is not just a marketing tool; it's a direct line to your audience. But it's not just about accumulating likes and shares. It's about engagement, dialogue, and community building. Use social media to tell your brand's story, showcase your products, and even provide customer service. With the right strategy, your social media platforms can become a valuable asset for your business.

In a rapidly changing business landscape, your ability to adapt is more important than ever. We've touched on the importance of a flexible business model, but let's delve deeper. Adaptability also extends to your workforce. Cross-training employees, encouraging a culture of continuous learning, and embracing new technologies are key. The market will continue to evolve; it's your job to ensure your business can too. Moreover, fostering adaptability in your organisation can also result in greater job satisfaction among employees, further contributing to long-term success.

## Strategic Partnerships: A Win-Win Game

Strategic partnerships can provide a significant boost to your business. By collaborating with another company, you can access new markets, share resources, and even improve your product offerings. But make sure it's a win-win situation. Both parties should benefit from the partnership, and it should be grounded in shared values and goals. In today's world, where news travels fast, maintaining a strong ethical foundation is not just good practice; it's good business. A single lapse can lead to significant reputational damage. Upholding ethics isn't just the responsibility of the leadership; it should be ingrained in the company culture. Encourage open discussions about ethical dilemmas and reward ethical behaviour.

### Innovation: Not an Option but a Necessity

Innovation is not just about new products; it's about finding new ways to create value. It could be a new business model, a new approach to customer service, or even a new way of conducting operations. A culture of innovation will keep your business ahead of the curve and make you more resilient to market changes.

### Crisis Management: Prepare, Don't Panic

In business, the unexpected is bound to happen. Whether it's a natural disaster, a cyber-attack, or a global pandemic, a crisis can strike at any time. Being prepared is your best defense. Develop a comprehensive crisis management plan that outlines roles, responsibilities, and procedures. Regularly update and test the plan to ensure its effectiveness.

In a crisis, clear communication is essential. Keep your team, stakeholders, and the public informed. Address concerns promptly and transparently to maintain trust. Remember, it's not the crisis that defines you, but how you handle it. Effective crisis management is also about post-crisis evaluation. After the dust settles, take time to assess what worked and what didn't. Use these insights to refine your crisis management plan for the future. Every crisis is a learning opportunity.

### Customer Retention: Beyond the First Sale

Acquiring a new customer is just the beginning; retaining them is where the real challenge lies. Customer retention is not just about offering discounts or loyalty programs, although those can help. It's about building a relationship. Understand their needs, exceed their expectations, and provide consistent value. Regularly check in with your customers through surveys or personalised messages. Keep them engaged with your brand through meaningful interactions. A retained customer not only brings in revenue but also serves as a brand advocate.

### Action Checklist
1. Conduct a thorough market analysis.
2. Develop a detailed business plan.
3. Secure adequate funding.

4. Choose the right business location.
5. Build a strong team.
6. Focus on customer service.
7. Implement effective marketing strategies.
8. Regularly review financial statements.
9. Maintain a strong online presence.
10. Continuously update your products/services to meet market demands.

### Final Thoughts: The Journey Ahead

Building a business that not only grows but grows profitably is a marathon, not a sprint. It requires strategic thinking, relentless focus, and a willingness to adapt and learn. But most importantly, it requires action. Knowledge is only power when it's applied. So take these strategies and actionable steps, tailor them to your unique business needs, and start executing. The path to profitable growth is laid one brick at a time, and there's no time like the present to lay the first one.

### A Personal Message from Manny Skevofilax

Thank you for investing your valuable time to read this guide. It's been an incredible journey for me, helping businesses transition from mere survival to thriving with profitable growth. The road ahead will be challenging, there's no doubt about that. But with focus, diligence, and a willingness to adapt, I have every confidence that you'll reach the pinnacles you aspire to. Remember, the best time to start was yesterday. The next best time is now.

**Connect with me**
https://evolvepreneur.app/s/manny

**Listen to Manny's Episode:**
https://evolvepreneur.app/s/eps06-46-1

Chapter 7

# SELF-COACH FOR BUSINESS GROWTH

**Tamara Pflug**

## About Tamara Pflug

Meet your Swiss confidence coach and fun ambassador, Tamara! If you're feeling STUCK in your life and your business and have tried everything on your own - but nothing seems to shift, coaching is THE solution for you. You don't have to feel powerless, helpless, and hopeless anymore.

Taking your life and your business to the next level AND having fun doing it is possible for you.

Many successful entrepreneurs build empires by shifting their mindsets.

The solution to a prosperous business isn't on the ACTIONS you're taking but on what you're THINKING right before taking any action.

The solution to a prosperous business isn't on WHAT you're doing but on WHO you're being.

I can help you with that!

You can have it all: A very successful business AND a very fulfilling personal life.

Let's make it fun and uncomplicated.

Today, not only professional athletes can get coached, you can too!

We live in the BEST time ever! :)

I can't wait to talk to you!

## Introduction

Hello, incredible entrepreneurs and visionaries! I'm Tamara Pflug, your personal fun and confidence coach, and I'm thrilled to guide you through this transformative journey towards business growth and personal fulfillment. In a fast-paced world brimming with challenges and opportunities, a mindful approach to business isn't just a luxury—it's a necessity. And that's precisely what this chapter aims to provide you with: a comprehensive guide to infusing mindfulness into every facet of your entrepreneurial journey.

Have you ever considered your mind as your most underutilized business asset? How often do you reflect on the ripple effects of your thoughts and decisions? Are you aware of the power of self-coaching techniques like the S.T.A.R. Method, or the transformative potential of positive affirmations? What strategies do you employ to overcome roadblocks that impede your business growth? How attuned are you to the financial aspects of your venture, and do you approach it with the same mindfulness as other areas of your business? Lastly, how often do you step into your customers' shoes, offering them not just products or services but experiences that resonate on a deeper, emotional level?

This chapter is more than just a collection of tips and techniques; it's a holistic roadmap to entrepreneurial success. From leveraging the untapped potential of your mind to adopting a mindful approach to team dynamics, financial decisions, and customer experiences—each section offers actionable insights backed by real-world examples and scientific research. So as you delve into this treasure trove of wisdom, I invite you to open your mind, engage your curiosity, and prepare yourself for a transformative experience.

So, are you ready to elevate your business and life through the power of mindfulness? Let's dive in!

## The Mind-Business Connection:

### More Than Just a Notion Your Mind as a Business Asset: The Untapped Goldmine

Your mind is not merely a repository for fleeting thoughts and half-formed ideas; it's a dynamic, living asset that can be continually refined and optimized for unparalleled business success. Think of your mind as fertile ground. Just as a farmer tills the soil, plants seeds, and nurtures them to harvest, so too can you cultivate your mental landscape to yield robust dividends in your business life.

The first step is to shift your mindset. Most people operate from a fixed mindset, seeing their abilities and circumstances as static. In contrast, a growth mindset enables you to see challenges as exciting opportunities for development, failure as nothing more than a learning curve, and success as a continual journey rather than a finite destination. This shift is more than semantic; it's transformational. It unlocks realms of possibilities previously shrouded by self-doubt and fear.

To start tapping into this untapped goldmine, consider adopting practices that promote mental well-being and cognitive excellence. Mindfulness meditation, for instance, has been scientifically proven to improve focus and reduce stress. Cognitive behavioral techniques can help you reframe negative thought patterns that often serve as self-imposed limitations. Gratitude exercises can enhance your emotional well-being, providing a more optimistic outlook, which is indispensable in business.

Investing in your mental health doesn't just improve your quality of life; it trickles down to every facet of your business. Improved mental clarity and focus enable you to tackle challenges with greater efficacy. A better emotional state ensures more harmonious interactions with your team, clients, and business associates. In the long run, a healthy mind can be your most invaluable asset, setting the stage for sustained business growth and success.

## The Ripple Effect: A Chain Reaction of Consequences

Imagine a single thought as a drop of water. On its own, it might seem insignificant, but the moment it falls into the vast ocean of your mind, it creates ripples. These ripples, in turn, generate waves that can either uplift or capsize your entrepreneurial ship. Each thought you entertain sets off a chain reaction that manifests in your actions, influences your decisions, and ultimately shapes the ethos of your business.

The concept of the ripple effect goes beyond mere cause and effect; it explores the interplay of thoughts, emotions, and actions in a cyclical pattern. A single negative thought can spiral into a vortex of self-doubt, leading to poor decisions and missed opportunities. Conversely, a single positive thought can inspire a domino effect of constructive actions, leading to beneficial outcomes for your business.

## The Power of Intention: Steering the Ripples

Being mindful of the kind of ripples you create starts with setting clear intentions. An intention acts like a compass, giving direction to the ripples you generate. For instance, if your overarching business intention is to provide unparalleled customer service, this will guide your thoughts, influence your business decisions, and dictate how you interact with clients.

## The Collective Ripple: Beyond Individual Impact

It's not just your thoughts that contribute to these ripples; it's also the collective thoughts of your team. As a leader, you set the tone, but each member's thoughts and actions contribute to the overall direction in which your business sails. Therefore, it's crucial to cultivate a positive, focused, and aligned team mindset to create ripples that move your business toward shared goals.

By being more mindful of the thoughts you entertain, the intentions you set, and the energy you bring into your collective business space, you can control the ripples you create. This enables you to steer your business consciously in the direction you desire, impacting not just your bottom line but also your company culture, client relationships, and overall brand image.

## The S.T.A.R. Method: More Than a Framework, A Philosophy

When you consider problem-solving, the S.T.A.R. (Situation, Thought, Action, Result) Method isn't just a tool; it's a philosophy. It's a comprehensive, 360-degree approach that allows you to dissect complex issues, explore alternative perspectives, and choose actions that are in alignment with your business objectives and core values.

## Situation: The Foundation of Insight

The 'Situation' element compels you to step back and examine the broader context in which a challenge or opportunity arises. This isn't merely about identifying a problem but about understanding its nuances—its origins, its impact, and its implications. What led to this situation? Is it a symptom of a larger issue, or is it a one-time anomaly? By thoroughly understanding the situation, you arm yourself with the knowledge needed to tackle it effectively.

## Thought: The Catalyst for Change

The 'Thought' element is the cognitive bridge between a situation and an action. It encompasses your internal dialogue, the beliefs you hold, and the attitudes you possess towards the situation. Are your thoughts constructive or destructive? Are they based on facts or assumptions? By scrutinizing your thoughts, you can uncover biases and misconceptions that may skew your judgment, allowing for a more balanced and informed decision-making process.

## Action: The Turning Point

The 'Action' stage is where the rubber meets the road. Based on your understanding of the situation and the thoughts you've entertained, what action will you take? Will you confront the challenge head-on, or will you seek alternative solutions? The actions you choose should not just resolve the immediate issue but also contribute positively to your long-term business goals.

## Result: The Mirror of Reality

Finally, there's the 'Result,' the outcomes arising from your actions. This is where you measure the efficacy of your problem-solving approach. Were your actions effective in resolving the situation? What were the unintended consequences, if any? Evaluating the results helps you refine your approach for future challenges, contributing to a continuous cycle of learning and improvement.

By internalizing the S.T.A.R. Method and making it a core part of your business operations, you create a reliable, replicable approach to problem-solving. More importantly, you cultivate a problem-solving culture within your team, making your business more resilient and adaptable in a constantly changing business landscape.

## Positive Affirmations: Not Just Words, But Catalysts for Transformation

## The Science Behind Positive Affirmations

Affirmations are not just feel-good phrases or motivational jargon; they are backed by neuroscience. The repetitive nature of affirmations serves to rewire your brain, gradually replacing negative thought patterns with optimistic beliefs. The brain's neuroplasticity, its ability to form new neural connections, makes this transformation possible.

## Crafting Effective Affirmations: A Step-by-Step Guide

Creating powerful affirmations isn't as simple as stringing together positive words. They must be carefully crafted to resonate with your unique circumstances, challenges, and aspirations.

**Be Specific**: General affirmations like "I am successful" may offer a quick boost but lack the punch to effect lasting change. Tailoring your affirmation to a specific area, such as "I am successful in scaling my business," not only focuses your energy but also aligns with your actual goals.

**Make It Present Tense:** Words have power, and the tense you use amplifies that power. Saying, "I will be confident," projects your desire into an uncertain future, whereas declaring, "I am confident," roots it in the present, making it actionable now.

**Include Positive Emotions**: Emotional words like 'joyfully' or 'enthusiastically' supercharge your affirmation. They add an emotional layer that resonates deeply with your subconscious, making the affirmation more compelling and impactful.

### The Daily Ritual: Incorporating Affirmations into Your Routine

Consistency is key when it comes to affirmations. Merely uttering them once in a blue moon won't yield significant results. Make it a ritual. Dedicate a specific time each day to consciously recite your affirmations. Whether it's the first thing in the morning, during your lunch break, or before bedtime, choose a time that you can stick to daily.

By adopting a disciplined approach to positive affirmations, you slowly but surely rewire your brain to focus more on your strengths and possibilities rather than your limitations and failures. Over time, this mental shift manifests in your actions, decisions, and interactions, propelling you closer to your business goals and personal aspirations.

### Overcoming Roadblocks: A Comprehensive Guide to Breaking Barriers

### Identifying Roadblocks: More Than Surface-Level Issues

Identifying roadblocks is an art and a science. It's not just about surface-level recognition of obstacles but involves deep diagnostic thinking. You need to play the role of a detective, piecing together various clues to get to the root of the issue. This entails asking probing questions:

What led to this situation? Is it an internal factor like a lack of resources or an external one like market conditions?

Is this a one-time issue, or is it a recurring challenge? Is it a symptom of a deeper, systemic problem?

What are the immediate and long-term implications of this roadblock? How does it affect your team, your operations, and your business growth?

Understanding these intricacies gives you a multi-dimensional view of the problem, making it easier to find a lasting solution. It also enables you to anticipate similar roadblocks in the future, equipping you with the strategies to mitigate them.

### The 'What If' Technique: Turning Fears into Stepping Stones

Fear is not just an emotion; it's a mental and emotional roadblock that can stymie your progress. The 'What If' technique is a powerful method to turn these fears into stepping stones toward success. It involves a two-step process:

**Identify the Fear**: The first step is acknowledgment. Write down what you're afraid of, as putting it on paper makes it tangible and less intimidating.

**Flip the Script**: For each fear, counter it with positive 'What Ifs.' For instance, if your fear is "What if I lose money on this investment?", flip it to "What if this investment doubles my revenue?"

### Turning 'What Ifs' into Action Plans

Once you've listed the positive 'What Ifs,' take it a step further by turning them into actionable plans. For instance, if one of your positive 'What Ifs' is about doubling revenue, jot down specific steps to achieve that—like diversifying your product line, optimizing your marketing strategy, or expanding to new markets.

By systematically flipping the script on your fears and turning them into actionable plans, you not only neutralize the negative energy but also create a proactive roadmap for success. Over time, this practice will inculcate a culture of resilience and optimism, where roadblocks are merely detours on the path to success, not dead ends.

## Financial Mindfulness: The Underestimated Powerhouse for Business Success

### Budgeting and Spending: A Conscious Approach

Financial mindfulness is not just about counting pennies or obsessively tracking expenses. It's a holistic approach that involves consciously aligning your financial decisions with your business goals, ethics, and values. Budgeting, in this light, is not a mundane, administrative task but a strategic exercise that reflects your priorities.

## The Mindful Budgeting Process

Begin by mapping out your revenue streams and fixed costs. Then categorize your discretionary spending into various buckets, such as marketing, R&D, and employee benefits. As you allocate funds to each category, ask yourself: Does this align with my business goals? Is this a want or a need? This mindful approach ensures that every dollar spent serves a strategic purpose, be it for growth, innovation, or sustainability.

## The Payoffs of Mindful Spending

Financial mindfulness fosters a culture of fiscal responsibility and accountability. By scrutinizing every financial decision, you not only optimize resource allocation but also enhance ROI. This disciplined approach can lead to increased profitability, reduced debts, and improved sustainability, giving your business a competitive edge in the market.

## The Three-Question Rule: Your Financial Filter

Before any expenditure, especially major ones, run it through a three-question filter:

**Do I Need It?**: Assess the necessity of the expense. Will it enhance your product quality, improve customer experience, or streamline operations?

**Can I Afford It?**: This seems obvious, but many businesses falter by overextending their resources. Even if an expense seems beneficial, consider its impact on your cash flow and overall budget.

**Will It Contribute to Business Growth?**: This is the ultimate test. If an expense neither fulfills a basic operational need nor contributes to growth, it's worth reconsidering.

## From Questions to Action

These questions should not be mere mental exercises but should lead to actionable insights. For instance, if an expense fulfills all three criteria, the next step is to plan its implementation meticulously. If it fails any of the criteria, explore alternatives.

By consistently applying this three-question rule, you not only make more informed spending decisions but also ensure that your financial strategies are aligned with your broader business objectives.

## Building a Mindful Culture: Creating an Ecosystem of Success

### Team Mindfulness: The Bedrock of Collective Achievement

A mindful team is a powerhouse of productivity, creativity, and collaboration. It's not just a group of individuals who are present in the moment; it's a synergistic unit that thrives on shared values, collective goals, and mutual respect. Mindfulness, in this context, transcends individual well-being and permeates the organizational culture.

### Leadership and Team Mindfulness

The journey to a mindful team begins with mindful leadership. As a leader, you set the tone for your team's collective mindfulness. Your actions, your communication style, and your decision-making process all serve as templates for your team. Regular team-building exercises that incorporate mindfulness practices can be an excellent way to introduce and normalize this concept within your team. These could include mindfulness meditation sessions, gratitude sharing rounds, or even team discussions centered around mindfulness books or talks.

### The Benefits of Team Mindfulness

Mindfulness enhances the team's collective emotional intelligence, fosters better communication, and strengthens interpersonal relationships. When each team member practices mindfulness, they bring a level of focus, awareness, and engagement to their work that is contagious. This collective mindfulness can manifest in various ways—from fewer conflicts and misunderstandings to higher levels of creativity and problem-solving skills.

### Mindfulness in Meetings: A Paradigm Shift

We've all been in meetings that seem to drag on forever, with little to no value addition. But what if meetings could be transformed into platforms for meaningful dialogue, innovative brainstorming, and decisive action? Mindfulness can make this a reality.

### Starting Right: The Power of a Mindful Minute

A simple but transformative practice is to begin each meeting with a minute of mindfulness meditation. This helps attendees to clear their minds, shed the stress or distractions they might be carrying, and focus solely on the meeting's agenda. It sets the tone for a more engaged, productive discussion.

## The Mindful Meeting Framework

Beyond starting with a mindful minute, the entire meeting can be structured around mindfulness principles. For instance, you could incorporate silent brainstorming sessions where everyone takes a few minutes to jot down their ideas without the influence of group dynamics. Active listening exercises could be part of the agenda to improve communication skills.

By making mindfulness an integral part of your meetings, you not only enhance their efficiency but also improve the quality of decisions made and the relationships between team members. Over time, this can transform meetings from dreaded obligations into opportunities for meaningful interaction and valuable outcomes.

## The Importance of Feedback: Your Business Growth Barometer

Feedback isn't just a tool for customer satisfaction; it's your growth barometer. It provides valuable insights into what's working, what needs improvement, and what needs to be eliminated. It's an opportunity for dialogue, a conversation that can lead to transformative business changes.

**Actionable Steps**: Your Roadmap to Mindful Business Success

**Daily Mindfulness Journaling**: Dedicate 5-10 minutes every morning to jot down your thoughts, intentions, and goals for the day.

**Implement the S.T.A.R. Method**: Use it as a framework for problem-solving in your business.

**Create a List of Positive Affirmations:** Choose affirmations that align with your business goals and recite them daily.

**Identify Three Major Roadblocks:** Use diagnostic thinking to understand their root causes.

**Apply the 'What If' Technique**: Use it to flip the script on any fears or uncertainties you may have.

**Incorporate Mindfulness in Team Meetings**: Start each meeting with a one-minute mindfulness exercise to set the tone.

**Track Business Expenditures**: Keep a detailed record of all business-related spending for a month.

**Regularly Collect Customer Feedback:** Use this information to make necessary adjustments to your business model.

## Frequently Asked Questions (FAQs)

*1. Is mindfulness really relevant to business growth?*

Absolutely. Mindfulness is not just a personal development tool; it has real, tangible benefits for your business. It enhances focus, reduces stress, and improves decision-making—qualities that are crucial for business growth. Beyond the individual, a mindful culture within your team can improve collaboration and overall productivity.

*2. Can the S.T.A.R. Method be applied to any business challenge?*

Yes, the S.T.A.R. Method is a versatile problem-solving framework that can be applied to various types of business challenges, from operational hiccups to strategic dilemmas. Its strength lies in its structured yet flexible approach, which encourages you to consider a problem from multiple angles before taking action.

*3. How do I make positive affirmations more effective?*

The key to effective affirmations lies in their repetition and emotional resonance. Choose affirmations that align closely with your business goals and personal values, and recite them daily. For added impact, visualize the successful completion of the affirmation while reciting it.

*4. What if my team is resistant to mindfulness practices?*

Introducing a new concept like mindfulness may meet resistance initially. The key is to start small—perhaps a one-minute meditation session at the beginning of team meetings—and gradually expand as the team becomes more comfortable. Also, make it a point to share the tangible benefits of mindfulness to address any skepticism.

*5. Is financial mindfulness just another term for budgeting?*

While budgeting is a component of financial mindfulness, the latter is a more holistic approach. Financial mindfulness involves being fully aware of your financial activities, making conscious choices that align with your business goals, and cultivating a sustainable financial strategy.

*6. How can I measure the impact of implementing these mindfulness strategies?*

The impact of mindfulness can be measured both qualitatively and quantitatively. On a quantitative level, you may notice improvements in productivity, employee engagement scores, or customer satisfaction ratings. Qualitatively, you may observe improved team dynamics, better decision-making, and a more positive workplace atmosphere.

**The Journey Towards Mindful Business Excellence**

As we come to the end of this enlightening journey, it's essential to pause and reflect on the transformative power of mindfulness in business. We've explored a multitude of facets—from the untapped potential of your mind as a business asset to the ripple effects of your thoughts and decisions. We delved into practical self-coaching techniques like the S.T.A.R. Method, the science and application of positive affirmations, and strategies for overcoming business roadblocks.

We also examined the importance of fostering a mindful culture within your team, the significance of financial mindfulness, and the impact of creating a customer experience that resonates on an emotional level. The actionable steps provided are not just theoretical recommendations but real-world tools designed to bring about tangible improvements in your business and personal life.

Remember, the journey towards a mindful business is ongoing. The strategies and insights shared in this chapter are not one-off tasks but continuous practices that need to be integrated into your daily business operations. As you implement these, you'll begin to notice incremental changes that collectively result in a significant impact—be it in the form of improved team dynamics, heightened financial acumen, or enhanced customer satisfaction.

So, as you close this chapter, don't consider it the end. Instead, see it as the beginning of a new chapter in your business—one that is marked by increased awareness, strategic mindfulness, and unprecedented growth.

## Personal Message from Tamara

To all the incredible entrepreneurs reading this, I want you to know that you are capable of extraordinary things. The tools, insights, and strategies outlined in this chapter are not just theories; they're practical steps towards a more mindful, successful, and fulfilling business journey. So go ahead, apply them, and watch as your business transforms in ways you've never imagined. Keep shining, you fabulous human!

Connect with me

*https://evolvepreneur.app/s/tamara*

Listen to Tamara's Episode:

*https://evolvepreneur.app/s/eps06-32*

Chapter 8

# CAREER BY DESIGN

**Tony Pisanelli**

## About Tony Pisanelli

Tony Pisanelli is a Career Transformation Coach, Author, and Speaker renowned for his unique approach to career development and his deep understanding of the evolving employment landscape. His journey through the corporate world, marked by several successful reinventions, allowed him to rise above the common pitfalls of job dissatisfaction and avoid the pain of job loss that struck many in his field.

Tony's passion for studying the minds of great entrepreneurs like Jeff Bezos, Steve Jobs, Warren Buffett, and Anita Roddick has deeply influenced his coaching methodology. His philosophy centers on adaptability, inspiration, and purposeful living in one's career. Tony believes that being energized and inspired by one's work, having a clear vision and purpose, and the certainty to make a greater contribution are essential for a fulfilled life.

In a world where job security is increasingly uncertain, Tony emphasizes the importance of not letting one's career drift aimlessly. He is a proponent of the idea that everyone can reinvent themselves, and that careers, like all aspects of life, have beginnings, middles, and ends.

Tony's own career began in accounting, a path chosen under parental influence. However, early dissatisfaction led him to seek broader business roles, moving away from being a 'little bean counter' to engaging more fully with the bigger business picture. This transition marked his first career reinvention, leading him to more fulfilling workdays.

Mid-career, Tony found himself as a business analyst, a role he felt made him dispensable and undistinguished. This realization prompted his second reinvention, transforming from a vulnerable generalist to a high-value specialist in risk management, a field that focuses on proactively identifying and managing problems.

In the latter stage of his corporate career, witnessing the devastating impact of job loss on colleagues, Tony began crafting a future independent of any employer. This led him to embrace his passion for teaching and coaching, adopting an entrepreneurial approach to his career. He believes that everyone has the skills and experience to thrive in their career's next phase, regardless of what it may look like.

Tony's message is clear: "You have the skills. You have the experience. It's all about defining your abilities and what is important in your life so you can thrive in the next phase of your career, no matter what that looks like."

Listen here: www.evolvepreneursecrets.show

Welcome to an experience that delves into an essential area of your life; one that provides a key foundation for the other areas – namely, your career. I'm Tony Pisanelli, a career coach and advisor with a passion for helping senior business professionals to advance their careers to greater heights.

A career is a vitally important component of our life. It provides the financial foundation to meet our basic needs for food, clothing, shelter, and health. Our employment status also allows us to satisfy some of the more pleasure-based needs such as travel, entertainment, and socialisation.

Yet, for many people, when you look beyond the pay packet, their working life is a demanding, overwhelming, and stressful aspect of their life. This is something that is constantly being confirmed by employment surveys and in observing people's demeanour while in their workplace. Listening to what people have to say about their work is another indicator. Only recently, I overheard one person at the end of his work shift say to a colleague, "Thank God That's Over!"

Those exact same 4 words reflected many of my working days, certainly in the early years of my career while performing financial accounting roles in a large organisation. My early struggles in a dissatisfying career, however, were not in vain. I turned this painful experience into an opportunity by becoming a keen observer of people, as they went about managing the 3 phases of their career journey. The beginning, the middle, and the ending.

While I didn't realise it at the time nor was it my deliberate intention, when my corporate days would eventually come to an end, career coaching became a natural extension of the next phase of my working life.

Through my highly focused observation over the years, I firmly believe people usually follow one of two career paths.

The first and the most commonly followed path is climbing the conventional organisational ladder where a person progresses through junior, senior, manager, leader, and executive roles.

The second ladder is what I refer to as the **Calling Ladder**, where the progression is from Job to Career and from Career to Calling. By the way, it is possible for people to climb both ladders simultaneously—often without them realising it.

As the core tenet of my career coaching is to help people progress to the Calling Ladder, it is this ladder I will focus on in this chapter. The Calling Ladder is brilliantly encapsulated in the **Christopher Wren Story**.

The 'Christopher Wren Story' centers on three bricklayers working on a construction site to rebuild St Paul's Cathedral after the great fire of London in 1666. One day, while on the building site, Sir Christopher enquired into the role and the nature of the work performed by several of the workers.

When asked about his work, the first bricklayer who was toiling away laying brick on top of brick, replied with a painful sigh, "I am laying bricks to earn a living." The primary motive underlying his work was to carry out his daily tasks to collect a paycheck to meet his immediate survival needs. (**The Job Level**)

When the second bricklayer was asked about his job, he answered with a bit more enthusiasm saying, "I am a building a wall." This reveals that he had a broader perspective — his work was both a means to an income but also, he was contributing to his growth by taking on more responsibility. (**The Career Level**)

The third bricklayer responded to the question with certainty and purpose in his voice; "I am building a magnificent cathedral!" This man had created a working life that transcended the basic and external motivation associated with a job for an income, power, and status to one that served a more noble endeavour. This endeavour, building a cathedral, could be interpreted by some as doing God's work, and it was sure to impact future generations. (**The Calling Level**)

Here we have a scenario with three men, doing the same activity at the same location and getting the same money, yet all had a different perspective on their attitude to their work.

### Why follow the Calling Ladder?

Earlier in this chapter, I referred to a conversation I overheard where one colleague said to another, "Thank God That's Over!" This reflects a common attitude towards the traditional Career Ladder. However, adopting the Calling Ladder can change this mindset. Many people, despite achieving great success, high salaries, status, and power in their careers, still find themselves wondering, "Is This It?" If you're experiencing this, transitioning to the Calling Ladder might be the solution. I made this change and now assist others in doing the same.

## My Career Journey

During my long corporate career, which began as a junior graduate accountant and subsequently progressed through more senior accounting and business titles, this traditional and widely accepted path lacked something. Identifying the answer to what my career was lacking became something I began to pursue by becoming a keen observer of how others went about managing their career.

One gentleman who I keenly observed was Perry, a fellow junior graduate accountant who began his career at the same time as I did. Perry and I were both essentially number crunchers in the first few years of our career, but while Perry thoroughly enjoyed his work, I felt like I was drowning in mine.

My early years were best described as repetitive, mechanical, and mundane. I found myself living a life of quiet desperation, to paraphrase American Philosopher Henry David Thoreau.

Much like the story of the bricklayers, how can two people doing exactly the same work have entirely different perspectives, attitudes, and feelings toward their work? The answer to this question was to come from me getting to know Perry's childhood years. As a young boy, Perry grew up on a wheat farm where he and his family learned the discipline of managing finances wisely.

By saving money from the good harvests to provide the reserves needed to get them through the poor harvests, the farm remained a viable concern year-on-year and it also kept the family fed. This is where Perry's love of money was born; he loved talking about it, learning about it, and having it— he was the money guy.

Perry's genuine appreciation for money gave rise to a career in accounting where he would deliver financial expertise. In contrast, my accounting career had a different origin story. I grew up as the eldest son to parents who immigrated from Italy in the 1950's. They came to Australia in search of a better life for themselves and the families they would go on to create.

In my later years, I've learned from conversations with people who grew up in Italy during my parents' generation and even after, about the prevalent discrimination in Italian society. This discrimination was evident in the way educated individuals looked down upon those who hadn't undergone the rigors of the Italian education system.

My parents grew up in families where financial circumstances meant their school years were cut short, which deprived them of the education they wanted and saw them being discriminated against by society.

When my parents and their many compatriots moved from Italy and went onto become parents, they placed a strong focus on their children becoming educated. My parent's expectations that I receive a higher education created several challenges for me as I was not the most intelligent among my school friends. I can still remember the day I told Martyn, a close school friend, I had made it to university, "you going to university? You won't last a month," was his resounding vote of no confidence.

Fortunately, through my strong work ethic and a determination to prove my doubters wrong, I was able to successfully plow through 3 years and gain a Bachelor of Business Studies degree. While this delighted my parents, it did create other challenges. In particular, finding myself in a career that I didn't enjoy.

## Defining Moments

As a career coach, a crucial element of my Career by Design System focuses on the significant impact that the Defining Moments of a person's childhood have on their career. When a child can pursue a career aligned with their natural inclinations and true passions, they are much more likely to enjoy a satisfying and sustainable working life. This is a key principle of the Calling Ladder.

As a young boy, Alex enjoyed tinkering with tools, watching construction workers and building things. At one point with his brother and sister, they built a cubby house under the family home. All was going to plan until their father found out and put a stop to their activity as he feared for the home's stability.

Nonetheless, Alex's defining moment of discovering his love for building led him to become a carpenter, then went on to own a building business and after exiting his business, became a teacher of young apprentices. In other words, he started as bricklayer one, became bricklayer two, and then went on to focus on the next generation as bricklayer three. As the 3rd bricklayer, he is responsible for priming the potential of the next generation of builders.

Alex's progression was not something that happened by chance but by Design. He always had a vision of where he wanted to be 3-5 years into the future, had an action plan to get there, and held himself accountable for achieving his career aspirations.

## Your Career & You

There is a favourite saying that is often applied to people who are employed by organisations. Namely, that they leave 80% of who they are at the front door when they arrive to work each day. This was very much true for me when I was trying to be an accountant crunching numbers. There was more to me not liking my work than just the undue influence of well-intentioned but not fully informed parents when it came to their children and their choice of career path. Quite simply, it wasn't in my character to work as an accountant, unlike the "Money Man" Perry.

As Human Behaviourist, Abraham Maslow wisely said: "A musician must make music, an artist must paint, a poet must write, if he is to be ultimately at peace with himself. What a man can be, he must be." Because Tony wasn't an accountant by nature, there was no way I would see out a 30–40-year career making numbers. A few years was one thing, but several decades would mean I would be at war with myself.

So, Tony needed to discover who he was and then make his career an extension of that. The answer would finally arrive courtesy of much soul searching, self-reflection and from listening to the perspectives of those around me. Don't you find it interesting that sometimes we can get so close to things that we can't see the obvious – in such moments, it's wise to listen to others. If accounting work wasn't my music, then what was?

Fortunately, working for a large organisation gave me the opportunity to take on more business roles such as benchmarking international competitors, investigating contractor compliance, and Total Quality Management. It was through these opportunities that I developed my business acumen, people skills, and I was allowed to train and mentor others. **Teaching had emerged as my music!**

Tony needed to teach to be at peace with his career.

## An Integrated Life

I recall a time in my career when my manager went on annual leave and delegated his responsibilities to me, in addition to my own duties. At that time, we were reporting to Adrian, the company's Deputy CFO. He was one of the most ambitious individuals I encountered in my corporate career. Adrian was determined to become the CFO and was unstoppable in his pursuit.

One evening, as I was packing my briefcase to leave the office, Adrian appeared at my office door and said, "Where do you think you're going? I'm not done with you yet." Eager to maintain my career security, I stayed until he was finished.

Although I didn't cherish that moment at the time, it turned out to be a defining moment in my career. Nowadays, there's a lot of emphasis on maintaining a balance between professional work and personal life. This balance is crucial to prevent work from becoming overwhelmingly dominant in one's life, which can lead to stress, burnout, and strained relationships.

In my Career by Design System, I aim to elevate the concept of work-life balance to what I term 'An Integrated Life.' This achievement is something only a few manage to attain. However, for those who do, their workday begins to shed the "Thank God It's Over" mentality.

Richard Branson, the founder of the Virgin Group, exemplifies someone who has seamlessly integrated his career with his life. His philosophy is encapsulated in his statement, "I don't think of work as work and play as play, it's all living."

Another example is an entertainer who spent over 50 years in show business. In a radio interview, when asked why he hadn't retired despite his long career, his reply was striking. He told the interviewer, "Because it's not a job." While listening, I was intrigued by his perspective.

The radio host, likely fatigued from early morning shifts, might not have grasped the significance of the entertainer's words. However, with my background in career coaching, I understood its importance, and it has since become a key principle in my coaching guidance.

I see my career coaching business as a wonderful opportunity to experience my love of teaching, continuous learning and remaining relevant in the world. Far from being an intrusion or hindrance, it enriches my life. The cherry on top is that I no longer have anyone asking, 'Where do you think you are going?'"

## Doing Something for Humanity

Returning to the three bricklayers in the 'Christopher Wren Story', the first two were working primarily for a paycheck, fulfilling their basic needs for survival and security as described in Abraham Maslow's Hierarchy of Needs. It was the third bricklayer who transcended these needs, moving beyond just a career to what is known as a "Calling" – making a purposeful contribution to something greater than oneself.

Moving from a career to a calling is profoundly rewarding for many, due to the meaning and satisfaction derived from making a difference in others' lives. However, this transition is a significant challenge for most. Unfortunately, for many, the leap is too daunting to make.

One of my clients once shared her desire to pursue her calling but was hindered by fear. I explained to her that fear is a common barrier, with worries about financial stability or upsetting family members being major concerns. This reluctance to pursue a calling often leaves people feeling a void and a sense of emptiness or despair in their working lives. I experienced this myself in a significant phase of my career, feeling a lack of meaning as my work didn't seem to be making a difference in someone else's life.

## Awakening the Entrepreneur

Earlier in this chapter, I mentioned Perry, a junior graduate accountant whose passion for his work was in stark contrast to my own experience at the time. Perry stood out as more than just an ordinary accountant; he was an aspiring business owner who played a key role in sparking my entrepreneurial spirit.

While many people tend to focus on short-term career goals, Perry was different. He had a clear 10-year plan and vision that guided his future, aiming for a significant degree of control over his career trajectory. His ultimate goal was to run his own accounting practice. Unlike traditional employees who simply work for a company, Perry ensured his work also benefited his long-term objectives. He strategically chose roles within the company that would develop his skills in taxation, budgeting, investment analysis, and financial planning, all critical for the future he envisioned.

This deliberate approach enabled him to transition from corporate employment after a decade. He initially joined an existing accounting practice, which he was able to take over once the previous owner retired. Perry's journey exemplifies how a long-term perspective and strategic planning can lead to fulfilling career aspirations.

Realising the effectiveness of Perry's strategy, I later adopted a similar approach in my career when I recognised my employer had too much control over my career trajectory, which wasn't in my best interests. I experienced several instances that revealed a predator-prey dynamic, with my employer in the dominant position. I distinctly remember a Friday afternoon when my manager invited me into his office to discuss my interest in taking over as the project manager for the Y2K initiative in our company segment. I accepted, unaware of the demanding nature of the role, which involved managing people who had to juggle their project responsibilities with their regular duties.

The project was a success, and everyone's significant contributions were acknowledged. However, I nearly found myself out of a job when my previous position was eliminated due to headcount reduction strategies, and the Y2K project concluded.

Fortunately, my consistent track record of strong performance bought me time to secure an alternate role within the company. I transitioned to Risk Management, a specialist discipline highly valued both within the company and the broader marketplace. Alongside this new role, I continued to observe career journeys and further developed my skills in coaching and mentoring.

I took another valuable lesson from Perry: the importance of actively working on your career while working in it. This approach gives you greater control over your future, preventing others from dictating your destiny. It's a crucial factor in fostering an entrepreneurial mindset and constructing a career tailored to your design.

## Designing Your Career Path

As we come to the end of this chapter, I want you to remember one thing: your career is yours to design. It's not just a series of job titles and roles; it's a journey that reflects who you are and what you value. The principles and the short stories I've shared are more than guidelines; they are important motivators to help you sculpt a career that is as unique as you are.

You have the power to create a career that not only brings you success but also joy and fulfillment. This journey requires introspection, courage, and resilience, but believe me, it's worth every step. I encourage you to embrace your uniqueness, to lean into your strengths, and to boldly pursue the path that resonates with you.

Remember, designing your career isn't a solo endeavour. Seek mentors, build a supportive network, and always keep learning. And as you progress, don't forget to give back and to share your knowledge and experiences with those coming up behind you.

I hope my story and the principles I've shared inspire you to take the reins of your career. To not just dream about a fulfilling career but to actively design it. Your career is a significant part of your life's story; make it a story worth living.

Thank you for joining me on this journey. Now, go out there and design the career you've always wanted – a career that truly reflects who you are and what you're capable of achieving.

## Get a Reality Check for Your Career

Are you ready to take the first step towards a career that truly resonates with who you are? It's time for a "Reality Check" – an opportunity to see what shape your career is really in.

I invite you to take our simple and quick online quiz to get your career score. This isn't just another quiz; it's a thought-provoking exercise designed to give you insights into the current status of your career.

In just a few minutes, you can gain a clearer understanding of where you are in your career journey and what action may be needed to strengthen your current and future employment position.

It's a starting point for introspection, greater awareness of the challenges you face and may prompt questions you have not previously considered.

Take this chance to pause and reflect. Are you on the path that's right for you? Could you be aiming higher, dreaming bigger? Let's find out together.

Go here to begin your journey to a career by design:
*https://thecareeradvantage.com*

Your future self will thank you for this moment of clarity.

Connect with me

*https://evolvepreneur.app/s/tonyp*

Listen to Tony's Episode:

*https://evolvepreneur.app/s/eps7-090*

Listen here: www.evolvepreneursecrets.show

# PODCAST GUEST DIRECTORY

★★ 🌿 ★★

Listen Here:
*www.evolvepreneursecrets.show*

Listen here: www.evolvepreneursecrets.show

# GROWTH

## Our Featured Guests:

**Brent Haumann** with Host Christine Campbell Rapin
Season 3 - Episode 22: "Moving From The Marketing Funnel"

Brent Howman discusses his journey from corporate executive to entrepreneur in South Africa. He started his own company 3 years ago after a portion of his previous business was acquired. His company has evolved from focusing on digital communication products to providing broader customer engagement services. Brent explains how competing against large vendors requires innovating to carve out their own niche.

An important part of his strategy was having clear conversations with his family and team about the challenges of entrepreneurship and setting expectations for the journey. Brent believes Africa is well positioned for digital innovation due to infrastructure challenges driving new solutions, and his vision is to build the most engaged companies on the continent.

https://evolvepreneur.app/s/eps03-22

**Larissa Soehn** with Host Christine Campbell Rapin
**Season 3 - Episode 35: "Books, Business, and Boundaries"**

Larissa is a best-selling author with works ranging from science fiction to self-help. She is the founder of Next Page Wellness Coaching, where she helps people write, edit, market and publish their own books. Currently residing in Canada, Larissa balances the everyday challenges and joys of motherhood and business.

For years, writing has been her favorite hobby and was fortunate enough to turn that passion and talent into a career. Now, focusing on helping others write stories to boost their businesses, Larissa has jumped in with both feet and dedicated herself to serving clients that are serious about growing their credibility and their businesses.

https://evolvepreneur.app/s/eps03-35

**Coco Dee** with Host Mechelle McDonald
Season 4 - Episode 15: "Gain Basic Financial Literacy"

Coco is a Tahitian-born, French-speaking, straight-talking Aussie - who has lived many lives. From corporate career and self-made property multi-millionaire in her twenties, to taking over her failing family business and learning how to come back from losing all said millions (because of her ego and guilt!) in her thirties. Business is her bread and butter. But her lifeblood? Is seeing incredible women grow in their business journey and overcome their old stories and paradigms.

If you're looking for a place to bring the work to the woo and make the inner work the everyday, grab yourself a carton of chocolate coconut water and get to know her. She is now the owner and shareholder of multiple businesses and her mission is for women and young girls all over the world to gain basic financial literacy.

https://evolvepreneur.app/s/eps04-15

**Roxann Smithers** with Host Mechelle McDonald
Season 4 - Episode 16: "The Ten Year Itch"

Roxann Smithers is a Founder and Managing Member of Smithers + Ume-Nwagbo, LLC. Roxann has a passion for working with entrepreneurs and small business owners. Roxann's practice includes commercial litigation, premise liability, construction, contract review/negotiation, and general counsel services, in various state/federal jurisdictions.

A Super Lawyers Magazine 2012, 2014-2016 Georgia Rising Star, Roxann Smithers and S+U team with the Access to Capital for Entrepreneurs, SBA, Emory Start:ME and Club E Atlanta to educate entrepreneurs. Finally, Roxann is a registered mediator focusing on business disputes.

https://evolvepreneur.app/s/eps04-16

**Naomi Mamiye** with Host Mechelle McDonald
Season 4 - Episode 21: "The Design of Your Life"

When Naomi found herself divorced with 4 kids- no income or family to lean on, she had to turn to her creativity to start a business. People laughed when she proposed to start the Naomi Mamiye Design firm. Instead of letting it bring her down, she used it as fuel to propel herself ahead and prove them wrong. With a specialty in healthcare, Naomi Mamiye travels across the United States designing hospitals, rehab centers, assisted living centers, drug rehab centers and corporate offices.

Today, years later, she is considered a leader in the field and constantly gets asked by aspiring designers for advice or to watch her work. A true leader creates more leaders!

https://evolvepreneur.app/s/eps04-21

**Lucas Thomas** with Host Mechelle McDonald
Season 4 - Episode 26: "Finding and Building a Community"

For almost a decade, Lucas Thomas has been helping people create wealth, generate passive-income, and ultimately become existence masters. If YOU need help building, implementing, and executing YOUR FINANCIAL PLAN, Lucas can help you make it all a reality.

Having years of expertise in Real Estate, Paper Assets (Stocks, REITS, Seller Finances, Note-Making, etc.), and Business Creation (Serial Entrepreneur.), he has a holistic knowledge that can help you build your Portfolio of Wealth without having to take on any unnecessary risk. If their is a yield, Lucas Thomas has gleaned it!

https://evolvepreneur.app/s/eps04-26

Listen here: www.evolvepreneursecrets.show

Podcast Guest Directory

GROWTH

**Lili-Ann Kriegler** with Host John North
Season 5 - Episode 3: "Learning On The Fly"

Lili-Ann is the founder of Kriegler-Education. She is a consultant, speaker and award-winning author of two books, 'Edu-Chameleon' for teachers and 'Roots and Wings' for parents.

A child and family advocate, she believes education transforms lives.

https://evolvepreneur.app/s/s05-03

**Manny Skevofilax** with Host Mechelle McDonald
Season 6 - Episode 46: "Profitable Growth Is Achievable"

Manny Skevofilax, a business consultant, discusses strategies for growing a business profitably with host Mechelle. He stresses the importance of understanding one's goals and capabilities before taking on too many projects.

Manny emphasizes that relationships with clients are critical for success, and business owners should focus on serving their clients and making them feel valued. Delegating tasks and not trying to do everything oneself is also important for growth.

Manny shares that taking on too much debt early on can be risky, and it's better to establish profits and relationships first before major investments. Overall, the podcast provides helpful advice on determining what level of growth is realistic and prioritizing client relationships for long-term profitability.

https://evolvepreneur.app/s/eps06-46

**Steven Jaenke** with Host Brian Silverthorn
**Season 7 - Episode 7: What's The Cost?**

Steve Jaenke has been involved in the digital world for over 2 decades. Seeing the power of SEO early in the market he pivoted his business to focus on assisting SME to understand and leverage the power of Google. He was a finalist in the 2021 & 2022 Global Search Awards, and is a recurrent judge for the Australian Web Awards awards.

https://evolvepreneur.app/s/s07-07IM

## Podcast Guest Directory

| Guest Name | Topic | Host | Season | Episode |
|---|---|---|---|---|
| Julian Van der Waal | The build, Demolition and Rebuild of Julian's Business Career and Himself | Christine Campbell Rapin | 3 | 6 |
| Abbie Richie | Take Massive Action, Daily | Christine Campbell Rapin | 3 | 7 |
| Karen Ford | Money Matters | Christine Campbell Rapin | 3 | 11 |
| Kimbi Marenakos | The Transformative Gift of Burnout | Christine Campbell Rapin | 3 | 12 |
| Britt Lefkoe | Scale Authentically Without Losing Trust | Christine Campbell Rapin | 3 | 13 |
| Jordan Willshear | Do Not Be Afraid To Pivot | Christine Campbell Rapin | 3 | 14 |
| Kez Wickham St George | Your Mentor & Book Reviewer | Christine Campbell Rapin | 3 | 15 |
| Tero Moliis | Why Keep Building Today? | Christine Campbell Rapin | 3 | 16 |
| Tara Whitney | School Assemblies Are Not Negotiable!! | Christine Campbell Rapin | 3 | 17 |
| Phil Pelucha | Stop Waiting To Be Discovered | Christine Campbell Rapin | 3 | 18 |
| Andrea Putting | Success Is Not Enough | Christine Campbell Rapin | 3 | 19 |
| Leslie Chen | How Not To Be Afraid Of Being Unique | Christine Campbell Rapin | 3 | 20 |
| Laurie Mabelis | The Art of Public Speaking | Christine Campbell Rapin | 3 | 21 |
| Anastasia Anselm | Living Your Dream Daily | Christine Campbell Rapin | 3 | 23 |
| Ayush Singhvi | Bring Your Start up Idea to Life | Christine Campbell Rapin | 3 | 24 |
| Cate Beresford | Growing Your Business On A Budget | Christine Campbell Rapin | 3 | 25 |
| Mel Lieber | Business Growth With Out Of the Box Finance | Christine Campbell Rapin | 3 | 29 |

EvolvePreneur® After Hours Show Vol. 1

| Guest Name | Topic | Host | Season | Episode |
|---|---|---|---|---|
| Kevin Dulle | Be Your Own Experience Designer | Christine Campbell Rapin | 3 | 30 |
| Karen Gibson | Breaking the Cycle of Anxious Parenting | Christine Campbell Rapin | 3 | 31 |
| Le-an Lai Lacaba | How To Hire & Train Your Second Brain | Christine Campbell Rapin | 3 | 32 |
| Bernadette Boas | Success is All About Head and Heart! | Christine Campbell Rapin | 3 | 33 |
| Joseph Lenard | Advance your career - Write a Book | Christine Campbell Rapin | 3 | 37 |
| Jim Schneider | Parenting in Hell | Christine Campbell Rapin | 3 | 40 |
| Melissa Carson | The Voices In Our Head | Christine Campbell Rapin | 3 | 41 |
| Dawn Cady | Pivot for Power | Christine Campbell Rapin | 3 | 42 |
| Frederick Cary | The Dream Business Builder & Founder of IdeaPros! | Christine Campbell Rapin | 3 | 44 |
| Lauren Coats | Launching a 6-figure Airbnb business in 2023 | Christine Campbell Rapin | 3 | 45 |
| Tamara Gabbard | Mindset Shift: Scale and Thrive | Christine Campbell Rapin | 3 | 46 |
| Nicole Hesse | Broke Bartender to $1M in 13 Months! | Christine Campbell Rapin | 3 | 47 |
| Harvey Castro | ChatGPT and Healthcare: What is the future? | Christine Campbell Rapin | 3 | 48 |
| Michael Kittinger | Using Leverage To Build the Life & Business Of Your Dreams | Christine Campbell Rapin | 3 | 49 |

Listen here: www.evolvepreneursecrets.show

## Podcast Guest Directory

| Guest Name | Topic | Host | Season | Episode |
|---|---|---|---|---|
| Shaun Banks | Go for the Adventure | Christine Campbell Rapin | 3 | 50 |
| Hilary DeCesare | Re-Imagining Personal and Professional Success | Mechelle McDonald | 4 | 1 |
| Adam White | Double the Value of Business in Less than A Year | Mechelle McDonald | 4 | 2 |
| Peter Christian | Becoming a Successful Entrepreneur | Mechelle McDonald | 4 | 5 |
| Tiffany C. Wright | Always Have Options | Mechelle McDonald | 4 | 6 |
| Kevin Ly | Not At The Moment | Mechelle McDonald | 4 | 9 |
| Tyler Leber | How to Push Past Barriers of Growth | Mechelle McDonald | 4 | 10 |
| A.M. Williams | Address Your B.S. | Mechelle McDonald | 4 | 11 |
| Jess Bargenquast | Your Thoughts After Hearing My Challenges! | Mechelle McDonald | 4 | 14 |
| Krista Martin | Slowing Down to Speed Up | Mechelle McDonald | 4 | 18 |
| Steve Bacon | 6-Figure Coaching Company With No Ads | Mechelle McDonald | 4 | 19 |
| Amit Tishler | When Passion Meets Reality | Mechelle McDonald | 4 | 23 |
| Veera Mahajan | Women Empowerment Through Education | Mechelle McDonald | 4 | 24 |

# EvolvePreneur® After Hours Show Vol. 1

| Guest Name | Topic | Host | Season | Episode |
|---|---|---|---|---|
| John Farrell | Why Do We Do What We Do | Mechelle McDonald | 4 | 25 |
| Christine Franklyn | Hitting Your Stride | Mechelle McDonald | 4 | 27 |
| Holly Hester | Mindset: The Beginner | Mechelle McDonald | 4 | 28 |
| Jaime Jay | Identify, Hire, and Cultivate | Mechelle McDonald | 4 | 29 |
| Magnus Carter | The Best Content | Mechelle McDonald | 4 | 30 |
| John Moody | Overcoming Adversity | Mechelle McDonald | 4 | 32 |
| Fitz Koehler | The Best Content | Mechelle McDonald | 4 | 33 |
| Chris Joyce | Start a Startup with Just an Idea | Mechelle McDonald | 4 | 34 |
| Katarina Koik | Small Tweaks to Giant Peaks | Mechelle McDonald | 4 | 35 |
| Mark M. Bello | From Attorney to Author | Mechelle McDonald | 4 | 39 |
| Jason Wojo | Get More Clients and Buyers Through Paid Ads | Mechelle McDonald | 4 | 41 |
| Thom Dennis | Gather Round, Men, It's Time to Talk! | Mechelle McDonald | 4 | 45 |
| Wally Bressler | How to Escape from the Prison in Your Business | Mechelle McDonald | 4 | 46 |
| Ray Martin | Life Without A Tie | Mechelle McDonald | 4 | 47 |
| Allyza Spivey | From Unknown to In-Demand | Mechelle McDonald | 4 | 48 |
| Jasmine Holmes | Food for Thought on Pricing and Creativity | Christine Campbell Rapin | 5 | 1 |

Listen here: www.evolvepreneursecrets.show

Podcast Guest Directory

| Guest Name | Topic | Host | Season | Episode |
| --- | --- | --- | --- | --- |
| Damian Andrews | Life Is Hard For Many, But Not Everyone | Christine Campbell Rapin | 5 | 2 |
| Richard Phu | Business Freedom Design | Christine Campbell Rapin | 5 | 4 |
| Michael Nuciforo | How to Quadruple Your Revenue in 12 Months | Christine Campbell Rapin | 5 | 7 |
| Sally Gimon | Selling Your Business with a Spendthrift Trust | Christine Campbell Rapin | 5 | 8 |
| Lyubo Kuchuk | Amazing Talents at a Fraction of Your Costs | Christine Campbell Rapin | 5 | 10 |
| Laura (LauraAura) Wallace | Creating and Aligned Business | Christine Campbell Rapin | 5 | 13 |
| Melissa Smith | Virtual Assistants | Christine Campbell Rapin | 5 | 15 |
| Danny Carroll | Terminal Cancer is a Misdiagnosis | Christine Campbell Rapin | 5 | 26 |
| Ian Westmoreland | Living Your Best Life | Christine Campbell Rapin | 5 | 31 |
| Maria Tan | Algo-Proof Your Business | Christine Campbell Rapin | 5 | 32 |
| Kim Graham | Money Management Foundations & Misconceptions | Christine Campbell Rapin | 5 | 33 |
| Steve Lewis | Bootstrapping, You've Got To Go To Work! | Christine Campbell Rapin | 5 | 37 |
| Alena Turley | Juggling Motherhood and Business | Christine Campbell Rapin | 5 | 39 |
| Alexis Haselberger | Do More and Stress Less | Christine Campbell Rapin | 5 | 41 |
| Elaine Mingus | Profit Over Passion in Business | Christine Campbell Rapin | 5 | 43 |
| Stephanie A James | Being Open to Saying Yes to New Opportunities | Christine Campbell Rapin | 5 | 45 |

| Guest Name | Topic | Host | Season | Episode |
|---|---|---|---|---|
| Sarah Banks | Creating and Growing a Business in a vulnerable Niche Area | Christine Campbell Rapin | 5 | 49 |
| Paul Claxton | Why Technology Is Not The Solution To Innovation | Mechelle McDonald | 6 | 1 |
| Connie Inukai | Starting a Business in Retirement | Mechelle McDonald | 6 | 4 |
| Gregory Shepard | Accomplishing Amidst Neurodivergent Conditions | Mechelle McDonald | 6 | 6 |
| Yuan Deng | Turning Leads Into Sales in Instagram | Mechelle McDonald | 6 | 8 |
| Denise O'Donnell | Striking a Balance as a Small Business CEO | Mechelle McDonald | 6 | 9 |
| Jeffery Davis | Creating a LIfe of Legacy, Passion, and Power | Mechelle McDonald | 6 | 19 |
| Richard Wray | Augmented Reality | Mechelle McDonald | 6 | 21 |
| Rick DellaRatta | Jazz Artist and Entrepreneur | Mechelle McDonald | 6 | 22 |
| O'tion VanOhm | The Trauma Of A $165,000 Launch | Mechelle McDonald | 6 | 23 |
| Jake Ryan James Diorio | Crypto Investing in the Age of Autonomy | Mechelle McDonald | 6 | 24 |
| Leks Vucko | Five Lethal Mistakes | Mechelle McDonald | 6 | 28 |
| Zach Lemaster | Turnkey Real Estate | Mechelle McDonald | 6 | 29 |
| Jane Nicola Douglas | Art For A Better Life | Mechelle McDonald | 6 | 30 |
| Kasey Anton | Community, Hospitality, & Success: A Recipe | Mechelle McDonald | 6 | 31 |
| Tamara Pflug | Self-Coach for Business Growth | Mechelle McDonald | 6 | 32 |

Listen here: www.evolvepreneursecrets.show

Podcast Guest Directory

| Guest Name | Topic | Host | Season | Episode |
|---|---|---|---|---|
| John Neral | Three Keys to Coaching Business | Mechelle McDonald | 6 | 34 |
| Paul Wrightson | How To Feel Complete | Mechelle McDonald | 6 | 35 |
| Karl Swanepoel | Overcoming Adversity | Mechelle McDonald | 6 | 36 |
| Carly Pepin | Adversity Sparks Inspired Movement, Growth | Mechelle McDonald | 6 | 40 |
| Desiree Stafford | Trust Authority, Grow Business Your Way | Mechelle McDonald | 6 | 43 |
| Eric Biggs | Rediscovering Comedy's Profound Impact | Mechelle McDonald | 6 | 45 |
| Chad Wittfeldt | Key Business Fundamentals and Partnerships | Mechelle McDonald | 6 | 47 |
| Doug Stout | The Community Culture of Franchising | Mechelle McDonald | 6 | 48 |
| Melanie Mitchell Wexler | The Accidental Entrepreneur | Mechelle McDonald | 6 | 49 |
| Baljit Rayat | Bedroom Actions Impact Business Decisions | Mechelle McDonald | 6 | 52 |
| Evgeniy Kharam | Soft Skills In Business | Mechelle McDonald | 6 | 56 |
| Richard Wray | My Story | Richard Wray | 7 | 1 |
| Justine Martin | Reinvention- How to Modify and Adapt | Richard Wray | 7 | 2 |
| Elaine Lloyd | You Can Heal Yourself Within | Richard Wray | 7 | 4 |
| Rhonda Dibachi | AI, Entpreneurs and the Manufacturing Frontier | Richard Wray | 7 | 7 |
| Sean Weisbrot | Scaling Businesses Through Automation | Richard Wray | 7 | 9 |

# EvolvePreneur® After Hours Show Vol. 1

| Guest Name | Topic | Host | Season | Episode |
|---|---|---|---|---|
| Kole Whitty | The Work In Your Business | Richard Wray | 7 | 10 |
| Dean Salakas | From Clown To Market Leader | Richard Wray | 7 | 12 |
| Corrine Ishio | Entrepreneur Soul: Balancing Passion & Business | Richard Wray | 7 | 13 |
| Catherine Velisha | Valuing Food Production | Richard Wray | 7 | 17 |
| Simone Boer | Hacking Your Way To Success | Richard Wray | 7 | 18 |
| Samantha Whisnant | No Experience, Six-Figure Business | Richard Wray | 7 | 19 |
| Elen Sentier | Ogres into Allies | Richard Wray | 7 | 20 |
| Allen Gregory | Walk Away Wealthy | Richard Wray | 7 | 23 |
| Mark Rosenfeld | Unique Experience: Create Your Business | Richard Wray | 7 | 24 |
| Manpreet Dhillon | Diversity and Inclusion | Richard Wray | 7 | 26 |
| David Corsini | Faith Brings Unwavering Success | Richard Wray | 7 | 28 |
| Seema Giri | Unleash Best-Seller Power! | Richard Wray | 7 | 29 |
| Prashant Pandit | Breaking Major New Markets | Richard Wray | 7 | 31 |
| Marc Kramer | Meeting Investors Virtually | Richard Wray | 7 | 34 |
| Anna Bartholomew | From Burnt Out to Brilliant | Richard Wray | 7 | 35 |
| Shiny Unsal | Boost Your Coaching Income | Richard Wray | 7 | 36 |
| J Haleem Washington | The Business Corner | Richard Wray | 7 | 37 |

Listen here: www.evolvepreneursecrets.show

## Podcast Guest Directory

| Guest Name | Topic | Host | Season | Episode |
|---|---|---|---|---|
| Anthony Blomfield | WHAT'S UPP | Richard Wray | 7 | 40 |
| Chris Hanna | A story of Re-Invention | Richard Wray | 7 | 42 |
| Jacalyn Price | Living Your Best Life | Richard Wray | 7 | 48 |
| Paul Daniels | Leaders Are Learners Too! | Richard Wray | 7 | 50 |
| Chris Anderson | No Plan 'B' | Richard Wray | 7 | 52 |
| Nicholas Kemp | Dealing with Impostor Syndrome | Richard Wray | 7 | 53 |
| Scott Montgomery | How Unconventional Success Can Be Yours Too | Richard Wray | 7 | 55 |
| Donna Groves | Wellbeing In The Workplace | Richard Wray | 7 | 63 |
| Andrew Wilner | Side Gigs | Richard Wray | 7 | 65 |
| Sandra Veledar | I.Liv, A Personally-Inspired Performance Program | Richard Wray | 7 | 70 |

# LEADERSHIP

## Our Featured Guests:

 **Robert White** with Host Christine Campbell Rapin
Season 3 - Episode 5: Been There and Done That

Robert White pioneered personal transformational growth in the U.S.A and Asia with over one million graduates from companies he founded and led. Today he is a Speaker, Leadership Trainer, Best-selling Author, Business Consultant and Executive Mentor.

Robert White was raised in poverty and with much physical and emotional abuse. Dropped out of college after one semester as a result of suffering the first of three heart attacks. He attended one of the early Human Potential Training events which helped him "get me out of the way of success." Went on to incredible entrepreneurial accomplishment and at least one spectacular failure. Retired at 46 to a 14,500 sq ft home in Aspen with his wife, the love of his life. Then lost it all — his business and his wife — with lots of learning from those mostly unpleasant experiences.

Now primarily works as Mentor to executives committed to living extraordinary lives. Returned in 2020 from six years doing leadership training and mentoring executives in China. Robert is once again engaged in a fresh start and loves working with extraordinary entrepreneurs and owners who want support in living extraordinary lives – personally and professionally. He has spoken before audiences of 15 – 8500 from New York to Las Vegas to Beijing and many place in between; presenting to associations, corporations, non-profits and Rotary Clubs from Aspen to Singapore. Robert authored the best-seller "Living an Extraordinary Life" available in English, Traditional Chinese and Simplified Chinese.

https://evolvepreneur.app/s/eps03-05

Listen here: www.evolvepreneursecrets.show

## Podcast Guest Directory

| Guest Name | Topic | Host | Season | Episode |
|---|---|---|---|---|
| Stewart Marshall | If You're Looking at the Technology, You're Missing the Point | Christine Campbell Rapin | 3 | 2 |
| Sukesh Tedla | Trustworthy Culture in the Digital World | Christine Campbell Rapin | 3 | 3 |
| Ben Eden | Showing up for those who need you most | Christine Campbell Rapin | 3 | 27 |
| Catherine Olivier | One size, Three Different Bodies | Mechelle McDonald | 4 | 3 |
| Sherry James | Creating Mental Millionaires | Mechelle McDonald | 4 | 13 |
| Blake Hutchison | When Is the Right Time to Exit? | Mechelle McDonald | 4 | 42 |
| Danielle D Pollard | Teamwork Makes the Dream Work | Christine Campbell Rapin | 5 | 9 |
| Sean Si | Cost to Scale Up Your Business | Christine Campbell Rapin | 5 | 25 |
| Titus Walker | Game Changers | Mechelle McDonald | 6 | 20 |
| David Kitchen | Laying Bricks: Building a Business Foundation | Mechelle McDonald | 6 | 38 |
| Liz Wolfe | Empowerment Keys for Entrepreneur Abundance | Mechelle McDonald | 6 | 54 |
| Sally Higoe | Lead Fully to Fully Live | Mechelle McDonald | 6 | 60 |
| Brad Young | Grout Repair Empire's Accidental Triumph | Richard Wray | 7 | 15 |
| Cathy Spaas | Thriving In The Spotlight | Richard Wray | 7 | 45 |
| Alexandra Terrey | Kindness in Action | Richard Wray | 7 | 46 |
| Angel Anderson | Embrace Shift, Thrive in Transformation | Richard Wray | 7 | 57 |

## EvolvePreneur® After Hours Show Vol. 1

| Guest Name | Topic | Host | Season | Episode |
|---|---|---|---|---|
| Jeff Skipper | Relevance, Resilience, and Revenue | Richard Wray | 7 | 58 |
| Michael Bremer | Boost Self-Belief, Surpass Average | Richard Wray | 7 | 61 |
| Nathaniel Evans | The Changing Forces of You | Richard Wray | 7 | 71 |
| CJ Flood | The Art Of Self Leadership | Richard Wray | 7 | 76 |

Listen here: www.evolvepreneursecrets.show

# MARKETING

## Our Featured Guests:

**John McGhee** with Host Christine Campbell Rapin
Season 3 - Episode 34: Behavioral Health Marketing Challenges

John is the owner of Webconsuls, a digital marketing agency specializing in healthcare. He's been in marketing for over a decade, and Webconsuls has been around since 1999. Outside of work he enjoys watching sports, doing Jiu Jitsu, and spending time with his children.

https://evolvepreneur.app/s/eps03-34

**Ryan Newton** with Host Mechelle McDonald
Season 4 - Episode 22: Scaling a Digital Agency with Smart Digital

Ryan is the co-owner of Smart Digital which is a digital marketing agency.

https://evolvepreneur.app/s/eps04-22

**Rick McCulloch** with Host Christine Campbell Rapin
Season 5 - Episode 11: Everything You've Learned May Be WRONG!

Rick is a Profit Acceleration Strategist with 20+ years of experience in driving business growth and profitability. He believes that businesses should prioritize profit over revenue and focus on providing value to customers. Rick's turning point came when he realized he needed help and guidance to succeed.

Now, his goal is to leave a legacy of helping entrepreneurs achieve abundance and success. He is focused on attracting his "dream 100 clients" and can be contacted through his website, attractmoreprofits.com, for assistance in improving profits.

https://evolvepreneur.app/s/eps05-11

**Goose McGrath** with Host Christine Campbell Rapin
Season 5 - Episode 44: Knowing Your Numbers is Key to Profitable Growth

Goose McGrath discusses how he grew his business from nothing to one of Australia's fastest growing tech startups. In the early growth phase, they faced many challenges including running out of money and nearly going broke. This taught him the importance of understanding the financials and having sustainable profits.

While fast growth is exciting, he realized he needed to shift to building a business that could last for the long run through developing efficient systems. The podcast offers advice on recognizing when a shift is needed from a "CrossFit" growth approach to a more sustainable "ultra marathon" model to find lasting success and enjoyment in business.

https://evolvepreneur.app/s/eps05-44

Listen here: www.evolvepreneursecrets.show

Podcast Guest Directory

**Paula Cherie** with Host Mechelle McDonald
Season 6 - Episode 44: Master Risk and Creative Brand

Photographer and entrepreneur Paula Cherie offers creative empowerment through her Power Breakthrough retreat, emphasizing the confidence-boosting aspect of boudoir photography. Paula underscores the parity of branding and marketing in business and advocates authenticity for brand building. She encourages embracing vulnerability as a path to growth, acknowledging the challenge of focusing amidst numerous business ideas. Paula highlights the significance of mindset over skills for entrepreneurs.

https://evolvepreneur.app/s/eps06-44

**Anthony Murphy** with Host Richard Wray
Season 7 - Episode 67: Grow Business Amid Tough Times

This episode discusses driving business growth in challenging times with guest Anthony Murphy, founder of digital growth agency Attention Media. Anthony gained experience in his family's business before starting his podcast and agency.

He emphasizes the importance of leaning into difficulties and finding opportunities during crises. Anthony explains how he grew his agency during the pandemic by shifting operations online and continuing marketing. Core values and communicating what a business stands for are also discussed as important for building trust.

Another lesson was preparing for difficulties and having fallback plans like what is often needed for farming. Cutting marketing budgets during challenges was identified as a common mistake as new customer acquisition is critical for sales. Anthony is focused on innovating and scaling his agency while providing new employment opportunities.

https://evolvepreneur.app/s/eps07-067

EvolvePreneur® After Hours Show Vol. 1

**Matthew Mason** with Host Richard Wray
Season 7 - Episode 77: **Leverage Your Expertise with a Digital U**

In this episode, Matthew Mason discusses the transition from horse racing to creating digital products using expertise. He emphasizes converting knowledge into videos, podcasts, and more. Various digital product types, lead generation, and visual models for webinars are covered. Tips include clarifying messages and starting with an initial product, expanding over time. A client example illustrates the shift from direct delivery to business management. The podcast addresses strategies for experts to share knowledge digitally.

*https://evolvepreneur.app/s/eps07-077*

## Podcast Guest Directory

| Guest Name | Topic | Host | Season | Episode |
|---|---|---|---|---|
| John North | "My Story" | John North | 1 | 1 |
| Sigrid de Kaste | New Ways to Stand Out in the Online Crowd | Zachary Davis | 2 | 1 |
| Steve Ardire | How to Scale Smarter, Faster, Better | Christine Campbell Rapin | 3 | 4 |
| Jaime Nacach | Giving Back | Christine Campbell Rapin | 3 | 8 |
| Jeremy Poland | SEO & Scaling Membership Products | Christine Campbell Rapin | 3 | 10 |
| Benjamin Jones | Add $100k of Sales | Christine Campbell Rapin | 3 | 26 |
| Dominick Montgomery | Digital Marketing and Advertising | Christine Campbell Rapin | 3 | 36 |
| Mike Boccia | Spider Man's Secrets | Christine Campbell Rapin | 3 | 39 |
| Brandi Kolosky | Aiming For A $2 Billion Fund! | Christine Campbell Rapin | 3 | 43 |
| Tracy Sheen | The End of Technophobia | Mechelle McDonald | 4 | 7 |
| Breene Murphy | Obsessed with Removing Barriers to Sustainable Investing | Mechelle McDonald | 4 | 17 |
| Michael Solomon | Profit from Disruption | Mechelle McDonald | 4 | 31 |
| Glenn Gardone | Produce Immediate Results and Massive Sales Growth | Mechelle McDonald | 4 | 36 |
| Nickie Cobble | Niching Down to Scale Up | Mechelle McDonald | 4 | 38 |
| Jennifer Glass | Quickly Grow Your Revenues the Easy Way | Mechelle McDonald | 4 | 43 |
| Jonathan Royle | Take A Trance on Success with Royle Hypnotist | Mechelle McDonald | 4 | 44 |

| Guest Name | Topic | Host | Season | Episode |
|---|---|---|---|---|
| Marcus Svedin | Measurable Results-Based Marketing | Mechelle McDonald | 4 | 49 |
| Shayla Nicole | From Web Design to World Games 2022 | Mechelle McDonald | 4 | 50 |
| Stephanie Mojica | Learning to Write | Christine Campbell Rapin | 5 | 3 |
| W.D. Kilpack III | Making It Work | Christine Campbell Rapin | 5 | 12 |
| Shawn Bayley | Quadruple Your Earnings | Christine Campbell Rapin | 5 | 14 |
| Mike Miller | Where's The Money?! | Christine Campbell Rapin | 5 | 16 |
| Lani Dickinson | Self-Led and Self-Made | Christine Campbell Rapin | 5 | 17 |
| Gresham Harkless | You Are A Media Company | Christine Campbell Rapin | 5 | 18 |
| Laura Sauter | Staying The Course | Christine Campbell Rapin | 5 | 20 |
| Tai Goodwin | Twenty Years of Online Marketing | Christine Campbell Rapin | 5 | 21 |
| Melissa Seideman | Former Teacher Turned CEO | Christine Campbell Rapin | 5 | 22 |
| Nichole Howson | Boundaries and Self Care | Christine Campbell Rapin | 5 | 23 |
| Rushi Adhia | The World of MVPs | Christine Campbell Rapin | 5 | 37 |
| Genevieve Piturro | Purpose Rocks Your World | Christine Campbell Rapin | 5 | 28 |
| Craig Andrews | Create an Unfair Sales Advantage | Christine Campbell Rapin | 5 | 29 |
| Brian Sachetta | Navigating Law For Publishing Success | Christine Campbell Rapin | 5 | 30 |
| Tiffany Hoeft | Success with Fierce Decorum | Christine Campbell Rapin | 5 | 34 |

Listen here: www.evolvepreneursecrets.show

## Podcast Guest Directory

| Guest Name | Topic | Host | Season | Episode |
|---|---|---|---|---|
| Marques Ogden | The True Power Of An Unbreakable Mindset | Christine Campbell Rapin | 5 | 35 |
| Lisa Byrne | Scaling a Successful Group Program | Christine Campbell Rapin | 5 | 36 |
| Annelise Worn | Scaling for Business Success | Christine Campbell Rapin | 5 | 46 |
| Stephanie Chan | Building a Business While Supporting Aging Parents | Christine Campbell Rapin | 5 | 48 |
| Emma Tessler | Lights, Camera, Action: The Power of Video Content | Mechelle McDonald | 6 | 3 |
| David Harris | How To Grow Your Business Fast | Mechelle McDonald | 6 | 7 |
| Zac Stucki | Cutting Through The Noise | Mechelle McDonald | 6 | 11 |
| Lori Konkler | Necessary Tool for Online Entrepreneurs | Mechelle McDonald | 6 | 12 |
| Abigail Tiefenthaler | Client-Getting Strategist | Mechelle McDonald | 6 | 13 |
| Linnea Butler | Adapt or Die | Mechelle McDonald | 6 | 15 |
| Margee Moore | Surviving A Recession | Mechelle McDonald | 6 | 16 |
| Sandra Nomoto | Conquering a Niche/Growing Industry | Mechelle McDonald | 6 | 17 |
| Racquel Collard | Build the Business and Lifestyle You Want | Mechelle McDonald | 6 | 18 |
| Drew Donaldson | Perfecting the Business | Mechelle McDonald | 6 | 25 |
| Shauna Van Mourik | Comprehensive Solutions | Mechelle McDonald | 6 | 26 |
| Amber Griffiths | Experience that Grows with You! | Mechelle McDonald | 6 | 27 |

| Guest Name | Topic | Host | Season | Episode |
|---|---|---|---|---|
| Braeden (Jett) Rhys (Black) | Understanding Yourself, Your Truth, and Identity | Mechelle McDonald | 6 | 37 |
| Daryl Fletcher | Thrive with Community Builder's Blueprint | Mechelle McDonald | 6 | 39 |
| Lorraine Ball | Been There, Done That! Now It's Time To Do It Again! | Mechelle McDonald | 6 | 50 |
| Peter Wright | Valuing Life Lessons and Overcoming Adversity | Mechelle McDonald | 6 | 53 |
| Michelle Nedelec | Business Ownership Secrets to Scaling | Mechelle McDonald | 6 | 55 |
| Lori Highby | Meeting Overload - Focusing On What's Important vs Urgent | Mechelle McDonald | 6 | 59 |
| Chris Loverseed | Gone To The Dogs | Richard Wray | 7 | 3 |
| Luisa Ferrario | Get Qualified Leads Coming to You | Richard Wray | 7 | 5 |
| Christina Kumar | Take Massive Action | Richard Wray | 7 | 8 |
| Deb Fribbins | Boost Success, Reduce Stress, Thrive | Richard Wray | 7 | 14 |
| Rod Williams | I Can Make You Grow | Richard Wray | 7 | 22 |
| Armin Kakas | Solopreneur's Commercial Analytics Journey | Richard Wray | 7 | 25 |
| Damian Kernahan | Understand Your Customers | Richard Wray | 7 | 27 |
| Vance Morris | Systematic Magic | Richard Wray | 7 | 32 |
| Nadine Heir | How to Write Wiser | Richard Wray | 7 | 38 |
| Anton Harrison-Kern | Justifying the Effort's Worth | Richard Wray | 7 | 41 |

Listen here: www.evolvepreneursecrets.show

Podcast Guest Directory

| Guest Name | Topic | Host | Season | Episode |
|---|---|---|---|---|
| Rich Kozak | Clarity: Your Solid Foundation | Richard Wray | 7 | 43 |
| Rachelle C Davis | How To Beat AI With Personality | Richard Wray | 7 | 47 |
| Amy Cook | Weathering The Storm - Being A Small Business | Richard Wray | 7 | 51 |
| Kent Lewis | Stay True and Achieve Growth and Happiness | Richard Wray | 7 | 60 |
| Joanne Tan | Brand Building | Richard Wray | 7 | 62 |
| May Silvers | Do You Have What It Takes? | Richard Wray | 7 | 66 |
| Paul Ramondo | Agency Success & Inner Game | Richard Wray | 7 | 72 |
| Brandon Willington | From Nightclub Promoter to Digital Agency Owner | Richard Wray | 7 | 73 |
| Alyson Shane | From Solopreneur To Agency Owner | Richard Wray | 7 | 74 |
| Christy Wilson | Scaling Businesses with Passion and Purpose | Richard Wray | 7 | 79 |
| Ken Jacobs | How To Keep Going In Times of Uncertainty | Richard Wray | 7 | 81 |

EvolvePreneur® After Hours Show Vol. 1

Listen here: www.evolvepreneursecrets.show

# MINDSET

## Our Featured Guests:

**Hugh Massie** with Host Richard Wray
Season 7 - Episode 6: Entrepreneurial Quantum Leaps

Hugh Massie, the Executive Chairman and Founder of DNA Behavior International, is a renowned Behavioral Finance Trailblazer and Money Energy Pioneer. With 40 years of international business experience, he helps individuals develop a growth mindset and a healthier relationship with money. Hugh's work has benefited over two million people, reducing their stress and increasing their happiness and success.

Drawing from over 4,000 scientifically measured behavior and money insights, he has authored books on mastering money energy, discovering financial personality, and managing leadership behavior. Through coaching and charity efforts, Hugh is dedicated to helping entrepreneurs unleash their potential, preserve wealth for future generations, and understand the connection between money stress and overall well-being.

https://evolvepreneur.app/s/eps07-007

**Rian Janan** with Host Christine Campbell Rapin
**Season 3 - Episode 1: Cut Through The Noise**

Rian Janan is a business loving, oat milk drinking, book nerd mum of three running a six figure small business from home. With a background in psychology, personal training and nutrition, she built Powerhouse Wellness to educate women on holistic health, wellness and fitness with disruptive mindset shifts at the forefront for long term lasting change.

https://evolvepreneur.app/s/epso3-01

Listen here: www.evolvepreneursecrets.show

## Podcast Guest Directory

| Guest Name | Topic | Host | Season | Episode |
|---|---|---|---|---|
| Felicia Williams | Crack the Code to Living the Best Life in The Second Act | Zachary Davis | 2 | 2 |
| Prati Bhatt | Drink Your Way to Wisdom and Health with Teaphoria | Christine Campbell Rapin | 3 | 9 |
| Jodie Nevid | How to Turn Epic (and expensive) Fails Into Massive Income Earners | Mechelle McDonald | 4 | 4 |
| Amy Sanders | Free From Being the Bottleneck in Your Business | Mechelle McDonald | 4 | 8 |
| Shaun Sunderland | Brands Evolve | Mechelle McDonald | 4 | 37 |
| Kyle Newell | How to Succeed In the Unconventional Way | Christine Campbell Rapin | 5 | 5 |
| Annette Morris | Elevation of Women | Christine Campbell Rapin | 5 | 6 |
| Robert Norton | Challenges of Scaling to $100M+ | Christine Campbell Rapin | 5 | 19 |
| Manohar Grandhi | How to Remove the Anxiety of Insomnia | Christine Campbell Rapin | 5 | 24 |
| Bek Paroz | Rejecting Norms for Innovative Paths | Christine Campbell Rapin | 5 | 40 |
| Robyn McKay | Understanding Energy and Frequency Significance | Christine Campbell Rapin | 5 | 42 |
| Darshan Chavan | Building a High-Performance Remote Team | Christine Campbell Rapin | 5 | 47 |
| Cindy Nicholson | Tips and Strategies for Growth and Success | Mechelle McDonald | 6 | 2 |
| Chris Miles | Fast Financial Results | Mechelle McDonald | 6 | 10 |
| Arian Adeli Koodehi | Entrepreneurship: Resourceful Obstacle Conquest | Mechelle McDonald | 6 | 41 |

# EvolvePreneur® After Hours Show Vol. 1

| Guest Name | Topic | Host | Season | Episode |
|---|---|---|---|---|
| Jennifer Longmore | Thriving in Serial Entrepreneurship's Rollercoaster | Mechelle McDonald | 6 | 42 |
| Chris Cirak | Are You Ready To Be You? | Mechelle McDonald | 6 | 51 |
| Antony Curtis | Lessons Across Life | Richard Wray | 7 | 16 |
| Mark Herschberg | The Future Of Content Engagement | Richard Wray | 7 | 21 |
| Moriam Adepoju | How To Achieve "The Impossible" | Richard Wray | 7 | 30 |
| Lynda Roth | Becoming a 21st Century Business | Richard Wray | 7 | 33 |
| Tanya Kunze | The Science of Abundance | Richard Wray | 7 | 44 |
| Katherine Pomerantz | How Your Big Idea Can Change the World | Richard Wray | 7 | 54 |
| Pete Lord | Believe Me, The Pain Is Worth It | Richard Wray | 7 | 56 |
| Jem Fuller | The Best Is Yet To Come | Richard Wray | 7 | 59 |
| Wayne Wright | Innovate or Die! | Richard Wray | 7 | 68 |
| Steven Howard | Focus on People And Achieve Desired Results | Richard Wray | 7 | 69 |
| Sam Laliberte | Never Settle - Creating Your Freedom Lifestyle | Richard Wray | 7 | 75 |
| Kyle Gillette | Thinking for Yourself in Business | Richard Wray | 7 | 78 |
| Melissa Ahlquist | Fighting Imposter Syndrome to Build a Successful Business | Richard Wray | 7 | 80 |

Listen here: www.evolvepreneursecrets.show

# STRATEGY

## Our Featured Guests:

 **Lyubomir Kuchuk** with Host Christine Campbell Rapin
Season 5 - Episode 10: Amazing Talents at a Fraction of Your Costs

Lyubo is an experienced leader in Global Operations, Supply Chain, Logistics, E-Commerce, Innovations, and Transformation. He excels in achieving results through transformative changes, innovations, and cost reductions. With strong skills in negotiation, communication, problem-solving, and time management,

Lyubo develops and implements strategies within budgets and deadlines. His business provides outsourced staffing solutions, aiming to expand their client base while ensuring higher wages for employees. Lubo envisions becoming a true HR partner, helping clients grow by offering more services and experts. Their effective candidate matching system boasts a 95% success rate in finding the right candidates for client needs.

https://evolvepreneur.app/s/eps05-10

**Chris Gensheer** with Host Brian Silverthorn
**Season 8 - Episode 26: Easier Than Raising It From The Dead**

The episode discusses Chris Gensheer's transition from pastor to marketing consultant and personal brand copywriter. As a consultant, his focus is helping entrepreneurs develop their personal brands. He shares his strategy of growing his own brand on Twitter from 0 to over 300 followers in just 9 days by consistently providing value-oriented content. Chris' ideal client is an entrepreneur or thought leader looking to help their audience.

*https://evolvepreneur.app/s/s08-26*

Listen here: www.evolvepreneursecrets.show

## Podcast Guest Directory

| Guest Name | Topic | Host | Season | Episode |
|---|---|---|---|---|
| Mary Silver | A feminine Way of Working - How to Scale to 6-Figures with Ease | Zachary Davis | 2 | 4 |
| April Porter | Accelerate Growth and Profits In Record Time | Christine Campbell Rapin | 3 | 28 |
| Jaylissa Lea | Adapting Your Biz to Web3 | Mechelle McDonald | 4 | 12 |
| Warren Coughlin | Authentic Value Strategically Delivered | Christine Campbell Rapin | 5 | 38 |
| Sam Rathling | Leveraging LinkedIn to Scale and Grow Your Business | Christine Campbell Rapin | 5 | 50 |
| Karie Soehardi | Direct and Purpose | Mechelle McDonald | 6 | 5 |
| David Fradin | The Five Keys to Product Success | Mechelle McDonald | 6 | 14 |
| Monique Cunningham | The Money Is In Your List | Mechelle McDonald | 6 | 57 |
| Ashutosh Malgaonkar | Applying Data Science to Your Business Strategies | Mechelle McDonald | 6 | 58 |
| Gregory Mohr | Real Freedom | Richard Wray | 7 | 11 |
| Rich Bontrager | How to Build a Media Empire As a Go-To Expert | Richard Wray | 7 | 49 |
| Carol Schultz | Talent-Centric Organizations | Richard Wray | 7 | 67 |

Listen here: www.evolvepreneursecrets.show

# SUCCESS

## Our Featured Guests:

 **Daniel Krynzel** with Host Christine Campbell Rapin
Season 3 - Episode 38: "I Had It All...And It Wasn't Enough!"

In 2008 the real estate crash took Daniel out and he lost everything. He turned to drinking and had nothing. He lost the house, the cars, the toys, the money, and worst of all...custody of his children. After he got sober he started back into business. He jumped back into the mortgage business and had massive financial success.

Searching for his purpose, he then became a Coach, where he trained Realtors on lead gen and sales. AND yet even after he had achieved all his goals and had all of the money he wanted (he had the house, the cars, the toys, the family life) he was still unfulfilled. He felt empty. This is when God stepped in...he told Daniel that his purpose was much bigger than what he was doing and that if he had the courage to listen to his direct guidance, he would be massively emotionally fullfilled and finally be living his true calling.

 *https://evolvepreneur.app/s/eps03-38*

**Tony Pisanelli** with Host Richard Wray
Season 7 - Episode 90: "The 5 Secret Keys to Future Proof Your Career"

Tony discusses 5 secrets to future-proofing one's career, including moving to a calling level where you cannot be replaced and continually developing new skills. Richard shares how he progressed from IT jobs to a career in media before losing his previous role.

Tony explains the importance of caring deeply about your work and acting entrepreneurially even as an employee. They stress staying on the cutting edge of your field through continuous learning. Richard ensures he learns about new AI developments daily.

Tony advocates designing your own career path proactively rather than leaving it to others. Taking control of your career was the overarching message.

Richard found their discussion on transforming necessary career disruptions as opportunities highly stimulating. Tony's upcoming book will further explore how to design fulfilling, future-proof careers.

https://evolvepreneur.app/s/eps7-090

| Guest Name | Topic | Host | Season | Episode |
|---|---|---|---|---|
| Simon Bacher | Secrets Of The App Business | Zachary Davis | 2 | 3 |
| Jody Glidden | The Art of Selling in The Era of Intelligence | Mechelle McDonald | 4 | 20 |

Listen here: www.evolvepreneursecrets.show

# OTHER BOOKS

## Evolvepreneur Secrets For Entrepreneurs

So you have decided to create a new business or maybe add an extra product or service. Perhaps you are looking for a seachange.

This is always the exciting part of your journey but you also need to be realistic about what is possible and what financial or physical barriers you will have getting your idea to the next stage.

Discover how to fast track your idea to startup without risking large amounts of capital investment. Learn how to create your own marketing strategies to quickly test your market and grow your idea with our 5 step system.

The startup stage is your foundation. If your foundation is shaky, then the whole concept will be unstable as well. Most people spend very little time in this area and never commit to a few hours to really figure out their big picture strategy. Don't be one of them!

www.evolvepreneursecrets.com

## Book Publishing Secrets For Entrepreneurs

Having a published book is one of the most powerful ways to gain authority in your industry.

It's the ultimate marketing strategy that sells itself. Discover how to write and publish your own book and get it into the hands of as many people as possible. Learn how to create a book around your business, or even launch a whole new business.

The great thing about writing a book is that it not only ensures that you get crystal clear on what you do, but also how you do it. The five steps that guided the creation of this book will save countless hours of your time.

Create it, conceive it, and publish it - all in less than 90 days. Then, evolve your completed book and become a #1 International Best Selling Author!

# OTHER BOOKS

## Internet Marketing Secrets

*"For any business to succeed in the current era using internet marketing isn't an option any longer, it's an absolute must!"*

The purpose of this book is to educate and encourage business owners and managers on the main aspects of internet marketing so that they can learn and apply the key principles along with traditional marketing techniques to literally leapfrog competitors whilst generating substantially more sales, profits, and cash.

Internet marketing has now become a necessity as part of your marketing strategies. Without internet marketing, it's highly unlikely your company can increase sales or revenue.

Discover many low- or no-cost internet lead generation tactics that you can begin using today to double your marketing results immediately.

https://evolvepreneur.club/show-book/B00MMI4Y96

## The Game of Squash

**The Game of Squash** is written to help beginners to advanced players get more out of their game and find ways to win more matches. We believe squash can become very addictive, but what a wonderful addiction!

Most players strive to improve, but lack of discipline or knowledge can hold you back. **The Game of Squash** is designed to give you an easy resource for all things squash.

Here are just some of the topics we cover:

• Who can play squash–a description of the game and what you can expect to get out of it

• A basic understanding of the rules

• How to choose the best squash racket for you

• Tips and tricks for improving your game

https://evolvepreneur.club/show-book/B018JXYRE4

# OTHER BOOKS

## AUTHORITY

Strategic Concepts from 15 International Thought Leaders to Create Influence, Credibility and a Competitive Edge for You and Your Business

JOHN NORTH
CHRISTINE ROBINSON
MATT SMITH
ADAM JOHNSON
LARRY MORRISON
CATHY FYOCK
ALLAN MCLENNAN
JENN FOSTER
DENISE GABEL
JASON B.A. VAN CAMP
MARK LEONARD
MELANIE JOHNSON
NATHAN JOHNSON
EVERETT O'KEEFE
GEORGE SMOLINKSI

#1 Bestseller

## EVERYTHING You Know About MARKETING IS WRONG!

How to Immediately Generate More Leads, Attract More Clients and Make More Money

**JOHN NORTH**

## AUTHORITY

Strategic Concepts from 15 International Thought Leaders to Create Influence, Credibility and a Competitive Edge for You and Your Business

In this book, you will find the collective wisdom of 15 international thought leaders, scattered across three continents and multiple industries, as they share their best strategies for building influence and authority.

Covering everything from video and print media to social media and consulting, Authority lets you inside the minds of experts who have built their own authority and helped countless others do the same. Whether you find yourself in a small business or large, virtual or traditional, you can benefit from the increased impact and success that comes with Authority.

www.authoritythebook.com

## Everything You Know About Marketing Is Wrong!

In this #1 Best Selling Book, we'll reveal the strategies you can immediately deploy that will enable you to out-think, out-market and out-sell your competition.

What we want to do in this book is to teach you a system for marketing your business... to a point where it becomes instantly obvious to your prospects that they would be an idiot to do business with anyone other than you... at any time, anywhere or at any price.

What most business owners will focus on is generating more leads at any cost but this isn't the best way to attract prospects to your business.

We can help you build a million-dollar or even multi-million-dollar business. Also, make sure you take advantage of the free bonuses in the book!

www.everythingyouknowaboutmarketingiswrong.com

# OTHER BOOKS

## The 5 Stages to Entrepreneurial Success

Entrepreneurs commit to "the hustle" because they have a much bigger vision for their future than the average person. But then, if they work harder than an average worker, then why doesn't every entrepreneur become massively successful?

The fact is, many entrepreneurs are making the same mistakes year after year. Learn what those are and how to avoid them in The 5 Stages To Enterpreneurial Success.

https://evolvepreneur.club/show-book/B0 72N3XWXY

## Podcast Secrets for Entrepreneurs

"Podcast Secrets for Entrepreneurs" is a comprehensive guide that equips entrepreneurs with the knowledge to leverage podcasting for business growth. It provides a step-by-step approach to creating, launching, and growing a successful podcast.

This book is filled with practical tips and strategies, covering everything from equipment selection and content creation to podcast marketing. It also offers expert advice on monetizing your podcast, turning it into a profitable venture.

Beyond being a technical guide, it serves as a roadmap to digital age success. It empowers entrepreneurs with the tools to create a podcast that resonates with their target audience and drives business growth.

https://evolvepreneur.club/show-book/B0 BQVBG948

www.ingramcontent.com/pod-product-compliance
Lightning Source LLC
Chambersburg PA
CBHW070809100426
42742CB00012B/2303